MW00892719

Know Hope

Finding Hope in Tragedy

Daily Devotions for Those Walking in the Valley

Tammy Conner Stearns

Know Hope: Finding Hope in Tragedy
Authored by Tammy Conner Stearns
6" x 9" (15.24 x 22.86 cm)
Black & White on White paper
228 pages
ISBN-13: 978-1533304629
ISBN-10: 1533304629

Printed in the United States of America

Unless otherwise noted, Scripture taken from the HOLY BIBLE, NEW
INTERNATIONAL VERSION. Copyright 1973, 1978, 1984 by
International Bible Society. Used by permission of Zondervan. All rights
reserved.

First Printing, 2017

Tammy Stearns
Project H.O.P.E.
1419 S Enterprise
Springfield, MO 65804
stearnstammy@ymail.com

Ordering Information:
Quantity sales. Special discounts are available on quantity purchases by
corporations, associations, and others. For details, contact the author at
the address above.

"Tammy Jo, I don't think that I have the words to express how your devotions touched and strengthened me...how it helped me grow in faith to see you and Travis live out true faith during your time of loss. You lived and wrote what I knew to be true, but had never witnessed anyone actually living so faithfully so soon after such a great trial and then continued to walk that walk everyday. Like I said, these words cannot express how deeply touched I have been by your walk of faith, and I have shared your story every chance I get. You and Travis (& Tae) have touched so many thousands of lives through your living testimony. Well done thou good and faithful servant!"

Karen Mahan....

"Your devotions have greatly encouraged me and comforted me. Definite blessing."

Marian Kilpatrick Garcia....

"Walking through the valley is often where we become closer to God because we are at our weakest. This is where His power is made perfect. These devotions allowed me to experience His power!"

Bryan Williams....

"Your devotions give me hope, like the wall says, each day. You remind me where my true strength comes from and where to go when I am feeling weak and in need. The devotions give me strength to face the mountains and to know I'm not alone. They are always a great reminder and I thank you for that dear lady."

Sherry Rusch....

3

"Beautiful!"

Pam Jolliff....

"Tammy the devotions have made me look at my world in a different way and have given me an ability to mesh God into my everyday life and activities. To see His love through the struggles of life."

Debbie Wentler....

"Incredible how God is using Tae's life.... with your gifted writing , providing His insights and profound truths..... you are an inspiration to all."

Jo Burden....

"My day is not complete without them!!"

Robin Kragskow Hoerning....

"Tammy Conner Stearns, you taught me as a mother how to walk through grief in such a way that glorified God. To read your most personal thoughts as you walked the road of Taellor's death brought me such comfort. Your words gave me encouragement for whatever I may face in the days to come. Thank you for being obedient to our God and giving Hope to all those around you."

Laurie Sutton Moudy....

4

"You gave me strength while I was going through a rough time in my life. Your words and scriptures you posted lifted me up and gave me courage to face another day!! I do appreciate your willingness to share your thoughts, prayers, hope and faith. You have no idea how many people your positive words and example encouraged and renewed. Thank you."

Vicki Luttrull Rhodes....

"It will be a treasure to so many!"

Mary Ann Lengyel....

"I will never forget landing in Nicaragua and being greeted by Taellor. I was loaded with a heavy backpack full of things for serving. Taellor immediately took my backpack off my back and placed it on hers. She had a BIG smile on her face as I explained it was too heavy for her. Needless to say, I made a connection with her immediately. As I watched her work, I have never seen a young person so gifted or humble in working with the people, especially the children. She was mature beyond her years. The love of Christ poured out of her, touching everyone she came in contact with. I know Taellor was what she was because of her mother, Tammy, and God. Tammy is so rich in everyway, and I am so looking forward to her book. Her writings have taught me much."

Tibby Martin....

Know Hope

A Daily Devotion for Those Who Find Themselves in the Valley

Thank you, to so many, who came beside us in obedience when we found ourselves deep in the valley. For those who are family of our faith that He has given us, without you, life here would look so incredibly different. I dare say that each person that opens this cover deserves their name on this page for you have been a part of our journey.

Thank you to Project H.O.P.E. and Ridgecrest Baptist Church for being willing to "step out side the box" and encourage and equip leading us all on a journey that only God could write.

Thank you to our staff at HOPE Central and Center of Hope that we serve with daily.

Thank you to my wonderful editors. Susan, Mary Ann, Sarah, Stephanie. God provided each of you to enrich the journey. Thank you for your obedience.

Thank you for those who continued to encourage me to write and publish this. As I have always said, these aren't my words but His. But, thank you, for without each of you prodding me along, this probably would not have ever came to fruition. Hazel, your phone calls of encouragement were treasured more than you will ever know.

Thank you to Sarah and Stephanie, for being that circle.

Thank you to Annie, "that girl", who will forever be imprinted on our lives. The very best friend that Tae could have had.

Thank you to Travis, Slate, Antonio and Devon for being willing to entertain this thought and encourage its fruition. Thank you to Devon especially who so patiently and not so patiently edited and reedited.

For our Father, who in His sovereignty created a journey that continues.

Taellor, your life's desire was to be a missionary and to impart hope to the children. Well done, dear one, well done. Gold stars all around.

Dedicated to the One who wrote the Words and the one who was obedient to His call on her life.

Forward

We all find ourselves in the Valley from time to time. Some valleys tend to be mere dips while others are crevices deep within our very souls. A life that once was, will never be again. Whether it be from a betrayal, divorce, death or any multitude of evil that we constantly battle against find ourselves reaching and clinging to the only Foundation we know to be true, our Heavenly Father. While the world would have us reach out to material things that will only dissolve in our grasp, our soul yearns for Him, for His comfort and His peace.

Our valley came in the form of the death of our only daughter.

We are a simple family, really. A husband, wife, four kids and a dog who have set out on a journey of obedience following God's call to serve as missionaries in Nicaragua. God called us here over ten years before the move would ever take place. Looking back, we know He was using that time to prepare us for what we would encounter here. We knew that our lives would forever be changed. We anticipated that our lives would never be the same again. However, we didn't foresee what would forever change the landscape of our family.

God continually demonstrated His faithfulness daily while we walked in obedience serving where He had brought us to serve. Our daughter, Taellor and son, Slaton were thriving. Taellor had graduated high school early in order to make the move with us to serve in Nicaragua. She flourished here. Constantly surrounded by children while seeking out the poorest of the poor, the seemingly unlovable. Slaton attended a private school and was adjusting well considering his world had completely changed as he knew it to be.

Serving with Project H.O.P.E., we each had our dedicated ministries. Travis serving as a liaison to the short-term mission teams and Director of Community Development, myself as Director of Women's Ministry and Taellor worked with the short-term mission teams and organized Bible Studies and activities for the children whose mothers were in our Women's Ministry Bible Studies. We were living the life that God had created us to live exactly where we were meant to be.

Little did we know that our lives would soon become a walk of obedience that would require us to stay focused entirely on our Heavenly Father. A path we did not volunteer to walk yet one in which we have come to know Him in a way we would have never known Him before.

We had been studying the book of Job in our Women's Bible Study at the city dump. We started studying it because it was a common belief to those in the group that "real Christians" didn't suffer. I will never forget the study on the Wednesday before our only daughter died. "It's easy to praise Him when all is well. It's easy to glorify and speak of His goodness when things are good. But what happens when, like Job, your children die? What happens when your only son or daughter dies? What happens when my only daughter, Taellor, dies? What happens then? We praise Him. Even then, we praise Him." Not knowing that just three days later, we would be met face-to-face with that challenge.

Our hope is that this journey will encourage those who are walking a similar path as ours. Death will come to us all until Christ returns so we must be prepared not only to depart from this world but to also be left behind. A year before Taellor died, she gave her best friend a journal. Within that journal, she wrote Scripture references that she instructed Annie to look up. Annie was with Taellor that day when she took her last breath and that night Anne opened the journal for the first time in earnest looking up each verse. It seemed as if Taellor was walking her through this nightmare that was a reality. God has walked before us and was preparing our hearts for what would lie ahead.

We share the verses with you to offer encouragement. The devotions that follow them were written daily after Taellor had passed. These Scriptures were not her life verses nor verses she held dear. I knew, as being her mother and her ministry partner, which verses were dear to her in her life. None of the verses that she recorded a year prior to her death were those. Rather, they were verses written for such a time as this. Each verse reminding us of whom He is, how we know we are His, what death is and where we go then concludes with how we, those left behind, should live. We pray for each of you. The world and satan will try to convince you that this is the end but it is not…your borders have only been expanded.

You can read this as a book from cover to cover, jump around, and use it as a devotional or however God leads you to use it. The first chapter covers those early days following the unwavering life as we knew it and is then followed by the Scriptures and daily devotionals as God walked us through the deepest crevice of the valley.

Praying for you as you walk amidst your journey through the valley. May you find joy through simple obedience.

Tammy

Part I

Her First Days in Heaven

June 14, 2014 3:46 pm

There has been a bad accident. A tree fell on Tae... Please pray. It doesn't look good..

The following are excerpts from Facebook posts as we slowly began to process what had happened. Missionaries in a foreign country, my husband was about ten minutes away from our home and I was across town preparing for a wedding in the city dump. Taellor, our 19-year-old daughter, had a rare day off from working in the mission field with the teams and was spending it at our home with her two younger brothers and best friend, Annie, who had just arrived in country two weeks before. They are raw and not edited just as the events unfolded were raw and unedited.

June 14, 2014 5:36 pm

Our Taellor left this world this afternoon. She was in the country that she loved, doing what she loved, serving the God that she loved. We believe that we each have a time here in this world and only God knows that time. We know that while satan will try to use this for evil as far as we are concerned this will be used to glorify the One in whom we serve, for those that serve with her here. In this place, we know that she was living life to its fullest. To its greatest and all for Him.

June 15, 2014 (early morning hours)

Every day. Every day, here, I was aware of the hundreds of ways that our children could be hurt. Every day. Yet, not one of them was how we lost our Tae. She was swinging on a hammock, the tree fell and hit her on the head. There was no suffering, no second guessing on whether or not she would have survived if she hadn't been here. For that, we are thankful. We have been continuously surrounded by love here with complete support both from the US and here and for that, we are so thankful. I have a difficult time sleeping tonight knowing that tomorrow morning will be the beginning of a new normal. A day without her here with us. We will bury her here in the land that she was called to serve in. We will continue seeking to find and love on the seemingly unlovable. Thank you for your prayers, love and support as we walk down a path we've never walked before.

June 15, 2014

While in this earth, we struggle with why yesterday, why? Why? Why? Yet, we know He wasn't surprised. He knew before she was conceived how many her days would be. We find comfort in knowing she lived them serving His people. Loving on His children. No regrets.

June 15, 2014

Slaton, our youngest, asked last night why Jesus couldn't raise Taellor from the grave as He did Lazarus. "I know He can," he said. But remember, Jesus wept after that for He knew that He was pulling Lazarus from the glory of heaven. As much as it's her, I would never want to pull her back from the glory she is experiencing today. I used to tell her after a rough and chaotic but incredibly fun ministry day that she earned gold stars that day. Tae, many gold stars. Many gold stars.

June 15, 2014

We knew the tragedies that could happen here to any of our children. We knew the many risks however, not once did I worry about how Tae was killed. She was in a hammock that was swinging, a tree broke and she hit her head. There was nothing that could have been done. We are grateful that we will not live with the what-ifs. What if she wasn't in a third world country? What if it was a better hospital? It was simply her time to go. She was with her precious friend Annie and the boys. She was where she loved to serve, doing what she loved to do in the land that God had called her. She was serving God with wild abandonment. Psalm 139 tells us that our days are ordained before we even spend one day on this earth. Our days are ordained. Her days ended yesterday. God knew that. He wasn't taken by surprise. He was with her. Satan will try to use this for bad but we choose to use it for good. She will no longer know a dark world, she will know longer stand on the front lines against evil. She will be standing with the King. Thank you for the prayers. Thank you for the continued love and support.

June 16, 2014

Today the question was raised, "What if we offend others by speaking of Truth and Salvation during this time? What if it seems like we are using Tae's death as a "platform" of sorts? This actually took my breath away because our lives, our very being, our sole purpose on this earth is to share the Truth. This very Truth is what Tae lived, breathed and taught every single day. Every single day. So make no mistake, there is a battle being played out whether you choose to engage or not. It plays on. Christ is the only trump card, of that I am certain.

June 17, 2014

Tae at the Blue Bird Special Needs Orphanage. We loved to see Tae do ministry but this is where I truly believe her greatest gifts were with Special Needs. She started volunteering at Camp Barnabus as soon as she could and then chose to serve in our Special Friends Sunday School class at Ridgecrest Baptist Church when she was in junior high instead of youth group. This is where we saw Christ in her. Patient, loving. She saw deeper than we could ever see. In her testimony for those who have not heard it, she talks of a girl name Rhonda who while she had CP and was extremely limited physically by the worldly realm, used everything she had to praise God and bring people to Him. When Tae experienced this while serving at Camp Barnabus, her life changed. From that point forward, she dedicated who she was and what she was to Him. When we visited the Special Needs Orphanage this week to deliver milk Tae had made me promise not to forget to deliver the week prior, they spoke of her incredible joy and consistent love towards the orphans there. May we all strive to see past what the world would have us see.

June 17, 2014

I love each one of you. We love each one of you. From the moment that this tragedy started to unfold, we were surrounded by God's people. Surrounded by exactly who needed to be here. God just brought them here. His provisions continually humble us. For those that know me well, I am sleeping deeper than I have ever slept. I may feel weak physically but I truly feel as if I could move mountains. We have been able to go to the places where Taellor and I ministered. Places where only Tae ministered and had been able to boldly share Truth. Yes, it is difficult, but in a way, it is not. I can't totally explain it but God's presence is the strongest that I have ever experienced it. Travis has started taking pictures that I will share later and it surprised me because, I am the typical picture taker but his response was, "How else can we describe the joy that God has given us in this life without Taellor here on earth". The boys are doing well. We have talked with them both and they know where Taellor is and they believe with childlike faith. I wish that I could come to each one of you personally and love on you as God is letting me love on those here. I know we have friends grieving around the world and while we hold dear your love, prayers and support, please don't grieve as the world would grieve for the world grieves as those without hope. We grieve as a people who believes, deep down believes, that Christ died on the cross for each of us so that when that day comes and we come face to face with death, as we all will, that we would find ourselves standing face to face with our Savior in paradise. But I believe there is more. It isn't about just securing eternal life. It is about living a life set apart. It is about living a life that is not self consumed but rather selflessly consumed. It is about living a life focused on Christ. Please do not strive to be like Taellor. While she was incredible and served in a way that rivaled my own wild abandonment, she was only human. Strive, my friends, to be Christ like. Strive to see the world as He does. Let it break our hearts, let it open our eyes. Let it create in us not only the desire to love our fellow man but a desire that can't be contained. A desire that overflows. Love, love, love you all. There is not sorrow here. There isn't. There is a celebration of a life that was well-lived and I say this with a full, overflowing heart.

June 18, 2014

While our loss of Tae on this earth is not near what Spafford experienced before he penned the words to this song, we stand with him in saying "It is Well With Our Souls". I know there is much hurt, confusion and even great anger surrounding Tae's departure from this earth. And while we miss her as a mother and father, we know that her time, her days were simply completed. Yesterday as I was able to comfort Hosea, one of the boys in the dump who is just heartbroken, I shared the reason why Tae was even here in the first place. It was because of her love to the Father and out of that came an obedience that was unyielding. As I began to explain the source of that love and the gift of it that is offered to us all, I could feel the tension, anger and brokenness leave his body. As I told Hosea, it doesn't take walking down an aisle, holding up your hand or even a pastor leading a prayer. It is the simple, yet the real, belief in your heart that God is whom you will serve.. He is your Lord. He takes care of the rest. I am quickly reminded that even the demons have knowledge of who God is. They even fear Him. The difference is Who will you serve. **So for today and tomorrow and the rest of our earthly life, there will be no anger or deep sorrow.** For we choose joy. As we, along with friends and family, bury Tae today in the land that she loved. We bury her with great joy as we know her journey in this world is complete.

June 18, 2014

Praising time in the dump today. For the last two days, one of the boys (preteen) has been just literally wailing in grief. Yesterday, I was able to share why Tae was the way she was. It wasn't Tae. It is Christ and that same unspeakable joy is offered to all of us. Today, he returned with the biggest smile on his face. This afternoon another of the preteen boys came to me with tears running down his face. These are tough, tough boys and again we were able to point him towards Christ and he accepted Him. Tae and I were just talking about how this generation (the preteen and teen) has been the most difficult to befriend and build relationships with, however in the last couple of weeks, God has opened doors. He's raising up a new generation. Love it!

June 18, 2014

With bubbles blowing in the wind, Travis and the Furia Santa guys lowered Tae's body to its final resting place. I love the realness. The crowd of people followed on foot to the cemetery. I can tell you that tonight was like the final layer of salve of healing. Our hearts were overflowing with joy by this time. Surrounded by the people who have become our family. God is good.

There was never a thought on where Tae would be buried. This was her home. God had called her here long ago and we had just brought her home. Every one of the people here she loved and they loved her in return.

June 18, 2014

There was concern from our families that we were alone during the time of Tae's death. We were never alone. God surrounded us by His people. By the very people that He had sent us to minister to, He sent to us. I have never been hugged with so much passion and shared sorrow.

As I look through the pictures of her funeral. There are so many emotions evident on the faces. The face of a father preparing to bury his only daughter, a grandfather grieving the loss of his only granddaughter, a grandmother grieving the loss of her only granddaughter, an uncle and an aunt grieving the loss of their only niece, three brothers at their only sisters funeral and me, her mother, with my only daughter are reminders of a life well loved. In obedience while we grieve, we choose to grieve not as those without hope but as those that have hope. We know without a doubt where Tae is. She is with her Heavenly Father in heaven and the song that comes to mind is: " There is joy in the suffering." And that is what this has been, a journey of obedience, a journey experiencing the provisions of our Heavenly Father in a way that we have never before and yet also a journey of human emotions that we have never experienced either. There will be a day with no more tears, no more pain, no more fear and what a glorious day that will be.

I have to share the story of the Chacos. Tae's chacos were literally falling apart and she had taped them with duct tape. We were thinking they would make it until Christmas in order to send them in to get them repaired. Secretly, Ashley and Annie found some Chacos that Tae had custom made for herself for fun online and Ashley ordered them for Tae without Tae knowing. They came in just in time to make it to her funeral.

The service was absolutely beautiful. After we finished the paperwork the night that Tae died, I told one of our colleagues that we wanted her buried here but he would have to organize everything. I told him that I couldn't do it. We were amazed. The day before the funeral, it dawned on me that we probably should have been making decisions and arrangements but everything down to every last detail had been perfectly planned by our family at Project H.O.P.E with the love of brothers and sisters. I can not put into words the perfection of that day. Just beautiful.

9

There was a message that needed to be said to the very people that God has opened doors for us to minister. I knew that they needed to hear it from me. It is one thing to have someone say, "It is ok," and a completely different thing to hear from the mother that It is ok and that it is well with our soul. In Psalm 139, God tells us that we each have a specific time on this earth. He knows the days of our time here before we are even born. Tae had 19 years and about 3 months. Her life wasn't cut short. She didn't die young. None of us are promised a specific number of years even though we "kid" ourselves by predicting life expectancies. Tae's time ended on that Saturday and we are okay with that. There are so many lies that the world will tell us and we wanted Truth to be heard. So that week of her funeral, we went to all of the areas that she and we ministered in and explained Tae's death with Truth. And, yes, sometimes tears ran down our faces but Truth was revealed as it really is. To God be the glory.

And this was God's explanation point!!!! This was simply whimsical Tae. There's a cool ministry that we have been privileged to get to hang out with a bit. Tae had tumbled and done gymnastics with them just a tad but looked forward to working with them more. These are tough boys, tough men, and their director called us the night before Tae's funeral and said that they had put together something for Taellor, a tribute of sorts. We had no idea when or how they were going to do it but it just so happened that as the van that was pulling Taellor's coffin through the crowd they had lined up to do their tribute. For Tae's gymnastics and dance history, this was the equivalent to a 21-gun salute. This was the moment when I looked across the crowd and found Trav's eyes and we both knew that, within a shadow of a doubt, God totally had this right down to this very "Taellorish" moment. Love you Capital Edge!

The procession to her burial place (not too far from the new community we are building) was unbelievable. Even though food was being served, everyone left to follow the casket to her final resting ground on this earth. Travis walked alongside the truck that I drove and when we reached the place we were surrounded by our Nicaraguan family. Just surrounded. As the dirt was placed over her coffin, Travis started shoveling and before long one of the men from the village tapped him out and started shoveling. I loved the sense of community.

10

They loved her just as she loved each and every one of them. On the way out, the family of the boy in the picture with Tae carried her picture through the village of Mateare. In honor. God has blessed us greatly. We've been asked by many people when Project H.O.P.E. will "release" us to go home. This is home and we will only be released by God, just as our Tae.

While the physical look of our family might have changed, our family has not. Tae is still Trav's and my daughter and the boys' sister. She just resides in heaven now. We have been greatly blessed by so many people that God has placed in our path. Blessed beyond measure. We are a real family, as you can tell by these pictures! Nothing extraordinary, nothing special, just a simple family following God through obedience and through this obedience finding joy that surpasses all worldly understanding.

June 18, 2014 (From Devon, our oldest son)

I haven't said too much since yesterday before the funeral, not because I am in deep grieving, but because I am truly overwhelmed in joy. We can sit and cry and mourn over what had happen or we can rejoice and dance. Since I have been down here, we just have rejoiced and danced. Seriously we have been worshipping and rejoicing, laughing and singing, the way God intended a death to be dealt with. What a celebration it is has been!!! So those who are sad, be sad no more! These past 4 days here have been nothing but beautiful and exactly what Taellor would have wanted. Taellor wouldn't want you to be sad right now. She would tell you to suck it up lol. She'd want you to Strive even harder with whatever you're doing! Keep your chins up and rejoice with us. Be happy with us. Love you all!!!

June 20, 2014

This morning, we say good-bye to one of our best friends and our oldest son. Yesterday, we said goodbye to a group of people that mean the world to us. And God is still faithful. I think a portion of me wondered if there would be a change as those God has surrounded us with return and we settle back into our life here. I can tell you that the strength that we feel inside continues to become stronger. Just as the initial shock of Tae's death left us momentarily breathless, the clarity of Truth has become stronger and stronger. Again, amazed and in awe at the magnificence of the Father that one of His very first provisions was to surround us by those who spoke Truth into our lives.

June 21, 2014

Doing what she was called to do in the dump in Ciudad Sandino. I knew she wasn't a materialistic kid. But I never realized just how much she was not, until this past week. Devon had asked if he could take a few of her things to remember her by. He was in her room for a long time, which isn't too surprising given the circumstances but when he came out he had nothing in his hands. We laughed because this was typical Tae. She wasn't the least bit into technology or things. I think she lost every cell phone she ever had, did Facebook rarely and just didn't really get into the trappings of today's material world. We did a family photo this week and were asked to think of something that was Tae's favorite to bring to have in the photo, what mattered most to her to hold in the picture. Without hesitation, my mind envisioned each of us holding up a Nicaraguan child because that was what Tae held most important of all. Reflecting back in Tae's life in contrast of my own: What are my treasures? I know what I would like to say are my treasures. But if I were to be called home today and left "unexpectedly" from this world. What would the person who looks at my things say I valued most?

With Tae, she stored little in this world. Always did. Travis has a favorite story of Tae when she was only about 6 years old. She had competed in a gymnastics meet and was only one of a few of them who received medals that day. Her best friend at the time was so very upset. As Travis was watching her without her knowing it, she walked up to her friend put an arm around her and gave her the medal. And that was simply Tae.

June 23, 2014

Every time I look at this my heart is filled with just pure love. Look at her face. As every mother knows the many faces of their children. This face, this very face, wow, leaves me speechless. Tae had an amazing last three weeks on this earth. She had an incredible time the whole time she was down here but these last three weeks she seemed to just literally glow. She served stronger, testified bolder and loved even harder than before. There wasn't a fastness to her but rather a lingering, a taking it all in. She hugged more than she ever hugged during these last three weeks. She's always been a huggy kid but she hugged even more, so much so that Trav and I were laughing about it. There were reminders from her such as the formula to Blue Bird, the pinatas needed for this week. These were gifts, preparations for what laid ahead, confirmation that nothing is by mistake or overlooked. She had no problem with laying down her life. She had laid it down long before we came here. Hosanna, Hosanna, Hosanna in the Highest. Hosanna, Hosanna, Hosanna in the Highest.

June 23, 2014

The perfect storm that without God's grace, without faith, without a peace that I am still having difficulty describing could have ended so differently. I want to share some of the details of Saturday that could have given satan delight in all of this. From the position of the hammock, to the tree that fell, to the swinging of the hammock, oh heck, we might as well throw in th the fact that we moved here at all, any of these reasons would have been place to have laid blame. Blame defined as the ability to take the hurt of an event, an experience and place it on someone else in hopes that we ourselves might be relieved of unspeakable pain. And yes, for a while, in the moment, we feel better. We feel that whatever wrong that had been made had been righted and that we, ourselves, have fixed it. But that doesn't fix it. It simply plants seeds of hate, of disappointment, of despair. The very first words Travis spoke when I first saw him with Tae's body was, "I am sorry." and at that moment in time, God spoke through me for it wasn't his fault at all. "This was simply her time. He has called her home." We've joked about it since that if Tae had been simply hurt, even hurt bad, I would have been as made as hell at him for the position of the hammock possibly or the integrity of the tree. But we serve a God that isn't surprised and doesn't make mistakes, Taellor's time on this earth was complete. All of her days ordained had been lived and He had called her home. It didn't matter the circumstances. Yet, He chose the place where she felt safest and freer. The very first word Slaton spoke to me were, "Are you mad at me?" But why? "I was the one swinging the hammock." Oh precious one, God has called her home and you were there to be a sweet witness to it. Yes, had she had been merely hurt, oh my, but God ordained those days, ordained for a reason and a purpose and her days were complete on that Saturday afternoon. Letting go of blame is simple yet, the hardest of all things sometimes to do. We have been given a specific time and purpose for this world today. People will hurt and disappoint us. They just will. True and complete lasting happiness will never be found in this fallen world. It just won't. There will come a day when there will no more tears, no more pain, no more sorrow and enough food and shoes for everyone. Until then, we live to serve the Lord. The Lord of Abraham.

We serve a mighty God. I'm not sure why God has prompted, actually kept prompting me to share this. But I pray that if you are given the chance to make a change, be the peacemakers if you are holding blame, trust enough in God to shoulder the hurt, He's got it, of this I am sure.

June 24, 2014

Today is Tuesday. As I pack my tubs to prepare to go to the girls at House of Hope and then the ladies at the Cancer Shelter, my prayer is one of provision. We ministered side by side, yet apart. I, the women, and Tae, the children. So, intertwined for God's purpose. Today, we step into the field to minister one man down. I know that God is faithful, I know that He has a plan, of that, I am thankful. Pray that the children will see Christ in all of this and that satan gets no part. As we step out in the arena today, may our words be that of Truth, our actions purposeful and Christ-like, our spirits calm and may God be glorified.

June 24, 2014

Today, with tears streaming and well meaning advice that we don't have to go today, God spoke to my heart. *Finally, be strong in the Lord and in his mighty power. 11 Put on the full armor of God, so that you can take your stand against the devil's schemes. 12 For our struggle is not against flesh and blood, but against the rulers, against the authorities, against the powers of this dark world and against the spiritual forces of evil in the heavenly realms. 13 Therefore put on the full armor of God, so that when the day of evil comes, you may be able to stand your ground, and after you have done everything, to stand.* So we simply stand today. We go obediently to those He has brought us to serve and covered with the full armor of God and we stand.

June 24, 2014

Driving into House of Hope, the skies were overcast, children walking in with downcast eyes. "Dear Lord.. Help me explain even to the littlest one what I so firmly believe. Help me point them towards you." As I got out of the truck, a beam of sunlight cut through the gray sky. Instantly, I felt the warmth that it brought. Again as tears welled in my eyes, I walked the path of ministry we did together. This day I was literally alone. Due to logistic issues, our team with translators were late even Claudia wasn't here.

Just me and my God. So with a deep breath. Can I just say, you know when you are in a place doing what you were created to do? Tae knew that. She lived that. Tae was so extreme that she pretty much refused to live anywhere outside of that. Without the help of translators today, God and I taught our first lesson together. I enlisted the help of two of the girls to help with the kid's group and it was good.

June 24, 2014

How do you impart hope to a group of women facing death head-on when your very own daughter whom they loved has just died herself? What do I say? Quickly God said, "Not you. Me." Death has always been the "elephant" in the room at the cancer shelter. Well, today we hit that elephant head-on. And God was amazing. It's simple really. As one of the ladies shared, "We are born and we die." Again, Psalms 139. Our days are numbered before we are born. We can choose not to think about it, we can choose to try to analyze it or not to believe it but the result is the same. Our time will come. For some of us, we may linger and have time to contemplate "what's out there" while others are gone in the blink of an eye. Thanks for the prayers and support today. God always provides and, truthfully, while this wasn't our "flashiest day ever" it was by far our most heartfelt.

As I shared with a sweet, sweet lady as she lay in her deathbed with no family that will come to visit, I caught the precious glimpse of someone being prepared to go home. As we imagined what heaven would be like, I saw that same sparkle in her eyes and smile that we saw in Tae during her last three weeks. Heaven wasn't surprised last Saturday. We were but God had been preparing her homecoming and of that I am sure.

June 25, 2014

I have to admit I drug my feet on this one. Actually was thinking that by the time we get there, it will be too dark and it's not safe so we will have to turn around. But as God seems to always do, it was lighter tonight in the dump than anywhere else. You would think I would learn to just expect this! As we turned the corner into the dump, the kids came running, smiling, laughing and full of life! These were kids a year ago that couldn't even sit together much less listen to a Bible story and crafts! But I saw it. The very thing I have been telling each of our groups, that while Tae was incredible, the joy she had, the love she displayed wasn't hers but Christ's and it was out in full force tonight! The women's group was more subdued. They know pain and they know death. Instead of "I can't imagine" they hug deeper and tighter as one who has walked that path. One of the ladies shared, as she was fiercely embracing her daughter that she couldn't imagine how she could go on. But God will give you what you need. Exactly when you need it. In this study, we were in the book of Job. All because a few of the women voiced that bad things don't happen to those who believe. I think we've covered that lesson well. Case in point. We live in an evil world, a decaying world and a world where we will never find true lasting happiness. We are often surprised when we are hurt or let down but we were never told this world would be easy or that in this world we will find peace. Actually it is quite the opposite. So, as we go about each of our days, where is our focus? Where is our communion with our Heavenly Father? Is it daily, hourly. Only on Sunday? Believers, where are we in this?

Are we like Job's wife. We take the blessings but when bad comes our way, we turn away? Just random thoughts but when I think of how quickly Tae's life ended, I want to be sure that when I stand face to face with the Father that I have been close enough to Him in this world that I will recognize Him in the next.

June 26, 2014

Reflection time today. I've had the most interesting discussion with God today. I think when you go through any sort of tragedy, there are moments when you think with utmost clarity and then there are moments when your thoughts are all jumbled. Today was a jumbled thoughts sort of day. Almost like I was trying to piece something together but couldn't quite get the borders. Until I realized that we should have known this all along. Not that she would have died almost two weeks ago but that she was going to die. She was. In the Bible it is all laid out from creation to the final days. And, yet, it still takes us by surprise. I remember the day she was born so vividly and I know at that moment we weren't thinking about when the end would be. Didn't even consider it. But if on that day, we would have looked into God's word for direction, we would have found examples on how to raise her and also that He knew her days before the day of her birth, an instruction manual if you will. Instead, we focused on the "worldliness" side of her birth instead of reveling in the holiness of her creation. We weren't believers at that time and saw the world completely different. We saw life completely different. Today, it seemed as if God was saying, "But I've told you all along. It is all there right in my Book. Immerse yourself more. Come and know Me more." Almost reminds me of teaching, when students seem taken by surprise by a test question only to find out the question is taken exactly word for word out of page such and such. We've got the greatest manual of all times. It's time to focus on God's word as direction for life instead of everywhere else. So when the hardships come that seem to test our strength, we can say, "I know that one. God told me so."

June 27, 2014

Time, it can be your friend or it can be your enemy. Yet, one thing for sure is that it is constant. The sun will rise and the sun will fall. A new day dawns. And God said that it is good. This past week has been an emotional week. A week in which we have been in each of our and Taellor's ministries during our regular Bible study times. While it has been a difficult time, it has been a healing time, time of fellowship and time of teaching. But as this week ends, we find ourselves looking at a ministry
in which the landscape has drastically changed. Throughout the whole week, we found ourselves turning to tell Tae something, looking to see Taellor in the village only to realize it wasn't her, standing in front of the very kids faces that she loved and doing a Bible study that she should have been doing. We came here as a family to serve and serve we did. We each had our own separate ministries, yet, they intertwined greatly. Our family landscape has drastically changed. Like the Christmas cards that I had yet to send out have now changed. As her parents, we loved serving beside her, loved seeing the joy in her life and loved seeing other people see her serve. She had a way about her that encouraged those who were apprehensive about serving would see and would find themselves jumping in with her. She served people in a manner that wasn't awkward but came directly from her heart. It is hard not to see that in person again. It is difficult to see new people on teams come and go that will never experience Tae as we did. These are worldy, fleshy emotions but real and raw. Today, as Trav was driving me to the airport we talked about how this season in our life is a season of pure obedience. Obedience. Moving to Nicaragua wasn't a sacrifice at all nor an act of obedience for us. It was the greatest blessing ever. Processing through Tae's death, refusing to fall to the worldly realm, eyes focused only on Christ is a strict act of obedience. **I know that it was simply her time that God ordained before even her birth.** And even though there are other "explanations" that might give worldly comfort, there is only one Truth. God didn't need another angel. He didn't need her work in heaven. Simply her time here was finished. .

19

As I sit in the airport waiting for my plane's departure, I find myself surrounded by a youth group who has randomly decided to surround me instead of the other million chairs available. As I hear their conversations, I realize even more how Tae was different, how she chose to live her life set apart. Obedience. Project H.O.P.E. has decided to name the Children's Center that will serve the same children that Tae loved after her. Still unsure of the name (Taellor's House-Casa de Taellor?), this house fulfills the dream that Tae always seemed to have. She said that she never felt like she would get married nor would she have her own children but she would have many children and that she did and will. Please pray for Travis as I travel to the US for Tae's Celebration of Life. Continue to pray for our wonderful staff at HOPE Central and pray for those that we serve that they might see.

June 27, 2014

Last night when Travis came home he told me about this. It is difficult loosing a child. I think it is even more difficult for a father to loose his daughter, his only daughter, the apple in his eye, rough and tumble, fearless daughter. And while we know and believe, even praise Our Heavenly Father, the flesh is hard. As Trav said last night, I didn't think it could ever happen to us. It just didn't even cross my mind as a possibility. God is faithful, of that we are sure. God's word is clear and it is that in which we will find comfort within. As the days turn to weeks and now our weeks are turning to months, I know that we will learn more about our Father's faithfulness in this. I think we, us so included, have created a world in which we believe we control or at the very least we are entitled to boyfriends, marriages, children, a good long life. Yet, there is nowhere in His word that this is said. Tae so knew who she was. I look back and think , "Wow. You really got it!" She knew who she was. So as we carry on, who are we? Are we ready to die? (I used to HATE that phrase!) but are we? There was no indication before the accident that Tae would die that day. None. For that, I'm grateful. There was no lingering or suffering, for that I am grateful.

When I was taken to her body, there was literally a Holiness surrounding it almost to the point that I felt like I had to ask God's permission to touch her. Holiness, dear ones. We can argue, try to explain and ignore all that we wish but there is no other explanation for what we have experienced. And, yes, it hurts but with it comes a message that literally I am having to "muzzle" myself not to be shouting out at the top of my lungs in the Dallas airport! We have been blinded into thinking that all is well and that we are infallible. The enemy comes in many forms, lies and deceit, my friends. Death is not to be feared but rather to be realized as being the necessary transition from this world to the presence of the Father. I do believe that God is there for that transition. We saw a preparation in Tae three weeks prior. Her journal entries confirm that. She was ready. She didn't know when but she knew Whose she was.

June 28, 2014

I do have to share this interesting comment/question: "Now, don't you regret moving to Nicaragua?" I had to hesitate before answering this one, not because it made me angry or sad, but rather because I didn't know where to start in order to explain by answering a resounding no. We were able to experience Taellor doing exactly who God created her to be, side by side, day after day. He prepared her stateside for this and when she was taken to the country that she was created to serve in, Wow. What a gift. We have seen God literally move mountains, heal people, reveal Himself in mighty ways. We have been challenged time and time again to follow in blind obedience with eyes steadfast on Him (such as now) only to find ourselves on journeys that only God could have created. Our daughter's faith grew in such a manner that from the moment she committed to come with us to the day she died that she not only believed in God but was life totally sold out to Him. Regret?

Not at all. Privileged and humbled that God challenged us many years ago to come know Him more, to come see who He is, to be in the world and not of it and while it has been in baby steps, each step we took was part of a well-laid journey. This is part of that journey and we completely trust in Him.

June 29, 2014

Incredible Celebration of Life for Taellor last night and what I loved the most was the Truth that was spoken. Truth. Not words that as humans we have created to make us feel better such as, "God needed another angel. She's gotten her wings. God needed her there because she was doing so well here." None of this but Truth. God ordained our days before Tae was born, that was her time. Death is not to be feared but rather anticipated as the moving from this world where evil abounds into heaven where God surrounds. That nowhere in the Bible does it say that God will give you more than you can take. Nowhere, because during the journey of this life, you will get more than you can take and that is when you lean on God and that is when you literally throw yourself at Him and say, "Can't do this. You do it." And He does. Every time. Truth as in what does a Christian Life really look like? When He says "Lay down your life?" What does that mean? It means so much more than praying before every meal and going to church on Sunday. God is faithful, time and time again, this is the message. We've created a world where we try to find things that are faithful but the only constant faithfulness is found in Christ.

July 1, 2014

I've been asked many times, "How do I know if I have what Tae had? I say I believe but I believe there is more?" I can only share my journey of faith and that I have seen to those close to me and to those that I continue to disciple. In James 2:19, we are told that even the demons believe and shudder. "You say you have faith, for you believe that there is one God. Good for you! Even the demons believe this, and they tremble in terror." We know that even satan believes in God. We see in Job in his conversation with God. We see how even, satan knows who God is believes in him but chooses not to follow Him. So when asked do you believe, and the answer is yes, well, then you fall in line with many others who simply believe but the question is: Who is Lord of your life? The old hymn goes, " I have decided to follow Jesus" not I have decided to believe He's God but to not follow Him. That means making some (or what some would call) radical changes in your life. Radical or what's really Christ-like. I think that's a key component that we are missing as Christ followers. That doesn't mean that you have to quit your job and move to Nicaragua as we have. It means that you become obedient to His call on your life. You lay it all down, all down, and you say, "Your will and not mine." It isn't easy. My family's life was a whole lot "easier" before we made that commitment in a "worldly sort of way" but joy was ever elusive until that point. We are all called differently. I remember going into the grocery store and hearing the guys working in the meat shop tell about the day (and they could totally pinpoint the day) when Travis found Jesus. He completely changed. He had "believed" many years before but there came a point when Christ said, "Will you follow Me? Who is Lord in your life?" It happened in my own life. I'm not saying that salvation is a two-part plan but rather it is more than just acknowledgement that He is God. I guess my question is: What sets us apart from the demons in James 2:19 that believe and shudder? This verse, this verse made my faith real.

This very verse brought me to my knees one night when I realized that my "faith" wasn't any different from the demons that believe. I said I believed yet was living my life for me and my family. I turned my life at that moment over to Him as Lord in my life. This is yours God, do as You wish. It has been the most incredible journey I could ever have imagined.

July 2, 2014

In 1 Thessalonians 5:1-3, we are told that The Lord will come like a thief in the night while people are saying "Peace and Safety". One of the things about Taellor going to heaven that Saturday, one of the things that literally took my breath away was experiencing the awesomeness of God in such a way that I was awestruck. The swiftness, the decisiveness of that moment that she was taken home. That power tangible here in earth. Even in that state of grief, it was so evident. Later as I have been pondering that, God reminded me that His next coming will be just as swift. So swift, so quick that as we realize it's happening it is already finished. Already finished. That's how it was with Tae. Already finished before it was realized, her spirit taken to heaven, disembarked from her earthly body. Within the wingspan of one quick breath. I've never experienced that before. (Granted the majority of this journey is brand new) but that decisiveness made me understand " to fear God". Not to be afraid but to fear Him. I have a new-found reverence in our Heavenly Father. I have been witness to his mighty power intertwined with the gentleness of feathers. He is returning. His Word is true. It will be decisive and swift. Are you ready?

July 3, 2014

This morning as I walked out to the car, I saw a glimmer of yellow at the hole where the tree that fell lay. Looking closer, I saw the most whimsical yet beautiful yellow perfect mushroom right in the center. My mind immediately went to Stephen Curtis Chapman's song "Out of Ashes Beauty will Arise". He wrote this song after his daughter was ran over in a truck driven by his oldest son. Their book is amazing. I don't look for signs for Taellor. I don't look to see her here or even in my dreams. My soul is at peace with where she is. But I am completely humbled by God's faithfulness. As Trav and I talked this morning, this had to be. Her preordained days completed and He has made it as painless as possible. Last night, God literally stopped Travis in traffic (which is so uncharacteristically at that time) but as he described it it was almost as if God was saying, "You have a choice. All in and joyful or all in and distraught. You pick how you will do this but I will be the same." And as he inches slowly to his destination, joy filled his very being. *"Out of the ashes Beauty will rise. And we will dance among the ruins. We will see it with our own eyes. Out of these ashes Beauty will rise. For we know joy is coming In the morning. In the morning Beauty will rise. So take another breath for now And let the tears come washing down And if you can't believe I will believe for you Cause I have seen the signs of spring. Just watch and see."* Stephen Curtis Chapman

July 6, 2014

So what about bad thoughts, the dark, evil kind that seem to lurk mainly at night? Fair question. Several years ago, I literally started trying to rebuke all bad thoughts from my mind, literally throwing it out before it can take any kind of root in my mind. No entertaining it at all! Rose-colored glasses, denial. There are a whole host of adjectives that could be put on this one I'm sure but for me it is simply staying Christ focused. Does it glorify God? That is the litmus test. Do I fail? Absolutely. And do I pay for it? Oh my goodness so not worth it, so not worth letting my mind take off on a tangent that is a lie, an evil lie meant to deceive and destroy. I also am very cautious about what I let my mind see and this falls into the horror movie side of the world. I've seen enough in reality that frankly seeing it on the big screen puts an image in my mind that I have difficulty erasing, so why even put it there? Also, not a Halloween fan. In fact, one of my favorite things of Nicaragua is that Halloween does not happen here! Yes, I know it is all fake and fun totally understand that but so can not get past what it was created for nor what others use it for. Yes, evilness abounds and celebrates that day also. So as far as Tae, do I let my thoughts wander? No. Do I entertain the what-ifs? Not at all. I focus on the words God has given us. We gave our lives over to Him long before this, long before the move to Nicaragua. This meant we believe it all and within His word there isn't any room for additions or subtractions.

It is amazing to me how God walks beside us giving us what we need right when we need it. The past few days, we spent time just enjoying being, playing, reading, resting. I spent time reading the second book in the series Divergent, one of Tae's favs, and I completely can see why! And a book called The Hiding Place by Corrie tin Boom. (If you want to read about finding God in times of evil. This is a good one. Reminded me again that while our surroundings might change. God and His people do not.) But during this time, God reaffirmed some things to me. He is not a God of "what-ifs". Never. Period. Our human minds love to play in the land of what- ifs. Yet, God is found in "what is".

26

During the times when we don't know what to do, we should follow in simple obedience. There were many times since June, well, actually since we turned our lives over to Him that I simply did not know what to do but He did. And all I had to do was be obedient. I didn't have to invent anything new or flashy. Just follow. In happiness, follow. In pain, follow. And probably the most poignant of all from these last couple of days was Him reminding me of what heaven was really like. In the past few months, I have found myself in tears at times over Tae not sharing in certain experiences that I knew she would just love. Teams that she loves to serve beside, children she loved to visit and love on and the list went on and on and then I found myself staring at the ocean with tears running down my face thinking that Tae would never experience this again and God, as He tends to do with me, quickly brought to mind what the ocean here on this earth really looked like. I saw the pollution, the lives lost within its crashing waves, the murder that happened not too far from the shores we were on and then it seemed as God was saying, "See the world as it really is."

Open your eyes to what you are really seeing, not through My eyes, but through reality. He softly reminded me then of heaven. In its entire glorious splendor, did I really mourn Tae missing out on anything in this world when she is experiencing a place that my soul aches for and my mind can't comprehend. How dare I even believe for a moment that this is worthy. It is all about faith. Do we believe or not? As we walk this journey, I have found myself at several crossroads or so it seems but I am beginning to believe that they are experiences that we travel upon that can be either used to strengthen our faith and those around us or can turn us bitter and discourage those He has sent to us. Praying to continue to be worthy of Him who has called us

Go Down, Death
James Weldon Johnson, 1871 - 1928
Adapted by Andy Thornton for Taellor Stearns' funeral
June 18, 2014

Weep not, weep not,
She is not dead;
She's resting in the arms of Jesus. Heart-
broken father--weep no more; Grief-
stricken mother--weep no more; Left-
lonesome brothers--weep no more; She
has only just gone home.
Day before Sunday morning,
God was looking down from his great, high heaven,
Looking down on all his children,
And his eye fell on Sister Taellor,
Living her life of love and service,
God's big heart was touched by her life.
He desired to give her the greatest reward bestowed on any of His
creation.
And God leaned back on his throne,
And he commanded that tall, bright angel standing at his right hand:
Call me Death!
And that tall, bright angel cried in a voice
That broke like a clap of thunder:
Call Death!--Call Death!
And the echo sounded down the streets of heaven
Till it reached way back to that shadowy place,
Where Death waits with his pale, white horses.
And Death heard the summons,
And he leaped on his fastest horse,
Pale as a sheet in the moonlight.
Up the golden street Death galloped,
And the hooves of his horses struck fire from the gold,
But they didn't make a sound.
Up Death rode to the Great White Throne,
And waited for God's command.

And God said: Go down, Death, go down,
Go down to Nicaragua
Down in Managua,
And find Sister Taellor.
She's borne the burden of this life long enough,
She's labored very well in my vineyard,
And she's done all I have asked--
She's made me very proud--
Go down, Death, and bring her to me.
And Death didn't say a word,
But he loosed the reins on his pale, white horse,
And he clamped the spurs to his bloodless sides,
And out and down he rode,
Through heaven's pearly gates,
Past suns and moons and stars;
on Death rode,
Leaving the lightning's flash behind;
Straight down he came.
While those were watching round her laying on the ground,
She turned her spirit and looked away,
She saw what others couldn't see;
She saw Old Death.
Coming like a falling star.
But Death didn't frighten Sister Taellor;
He looked to her like a welcome friend.
And her soul whispered: I'm going home,
Her heart smiled and her body rested.
And Death took her up like a baby,
And she lay in his icy arms,
But she didn't feel any chill.
And death began to ride again--
Up beyond the evening star,
Into the glittering light of glory,
On to the Great White Throne.
And there he laid Sister Taellor
On the loving lap of Jesus.

And Jesus took his own hand and wiped away her tears,
And he brushed back the hair from her face,

And the angels sang a little song,
And Jesus rocked her in his arms,
And kept on saying: Take your rest, sweet Taellor
Take your rest.
Weep not--weep not,
She is not dead;
She's resting in the arms of Jesus.

Part II

The Scriptures

A year ago, Taellor had me buy a journal from the market for her best friend's Annie's birthday. Saturday night at Tae's Celebration of Life, Annie handed me a sheet of paper and on it were the scripture references that Tae wrote on top of each of the pages to encourage Annie to read her Bible more. Annie hadn't read them yet but had brought her journal with her for the summer she was to spend serving with Taellor. The night that Tae died Annie pulled out the journal and started looking up the verses. When I heard the significance of the scriptures, I thought in my mind that I could probably list the majority of them. I knew her favorite verses and those of significance in our ministries. When I looked at the references, I didn't recognize them. I'd love to share them with you. As Annie said, she was looking them up that night and it was as if Tae was right there with her explaining exactly what had happened and encouraging her in that God has this. When I read them I knew it was another provision from our Father.

A year ago, Tae wrote out the scripture references that would encourage and comfort us as we began our walk through the valley. As I wrote each devotion, I caught a closer glimpse at our Father and the foundation upon which our faith is built upon.

God is simply faithful. To know Him is to know Hope.

The Scriptures

Ecclesiastes 3:14

Ecclesiastes 3:20-22

Ecclesiastes 5:2

John 1:12-13

Acts 2:25-28

Acts 4:12

Romans 8:1-4

Romans 8:31-32

Hebrews 11:1-3

James 2:26

1 Peter 3:3-4

All of First and Second Peter

The Devotions

God Endures Forever Ecclesiastes 3:14, 20-22

I know everything God does will endure forever; nothing can be added to it and nothing taken from it. God does it so that people will fear him.

All go to the same place; all come from dust, and to dust all return. Who knows if the human spirit rises upward and if the spirit of the animal goes down into the earth? So I saw that there is nothing better for a person than to enjoy their work, because that is their lot. For who can bring them to see what will happen after them?

Incredible, isn't it? We know God was in this from the beginning, but these references written over a year ago still humble us; they point to His tenderness in comforting His children.

Many times, we plan ahead for the future by focusing on material things and overlooking spiritual preparation. The foundation was being laid as Tae referenced scriptures which would not only comfort, but also remind those of us left on earth that our work was not done: "I encourage you to read them, draw comfort and encouragement from them. Act on them."

Even amidst the valley, our work continues. Satan would have us sulk in despair and focus on ourselves. He would encourage a pity party. But there is no time for that, the battle rages on. So with bleeding battle scars and tear-stained faces, we pull ourselves up and we carry on.

Choose to Glorify Ecclesiastes 5:2

Do not be quick with your mouth, do not be hasty in your heart to utter anything before God. God is in heaven and you are on earth, so let your words be few.

Yes, life can be bad. Yes, it can hurt. But I will not give the world the satisfaction. I will not give satan the satisfaction. I choose to glorify Him in all circumstances. All circumstances. Every word. He is worth more than that. He just is. We can choose to let life's distractions taint our world. We can allow the chaos to come inside us, to cause us continued pain and despair because it is the world's reality in which we physically live. We can choose to focus on the craziness of this world and wallow justifiably, and few will admonish us; others will come alongside us and wallow with us.

Or, we can choose to see it is as it truly is. Smokescreen and mirages planted by Satan to create distraction and destruction. We are not part of this world. We are simply here as travelers on a journey. Some of us will become stuck in our journey. We will plant ourselves where we have fallen and we will stay there.

I refuse to rot, stuck in this world.

We don't have to. We have the power within us to choose differently. Be different. We can choose to make changes. Yes, the world will criticize because it simply doesn't understand. Many will not understand. They will accuse us of wearing "rose-colored glasses," of being deceived, or being in shock or simply out of touch with reality.

Yet, we live in a reality that causes this world to pale in comparison.

36

The world may see the reality of a young girl's life cut short before her time when, in truth, her time on planet earth was completed and she was called home. The world will speak of all that she will miss on this earth when, in reality, she will no longer walk amongst the evil of this world.

No harm will ever fall upon her again. The world may see a family broken when, in reality, we are a family whose borders have simply been extended. The world may expect us to question our Father's timing when, in reality, He told us from the beginning that our days here are numbered. There are some who will encourage us to publicly share our grief more, to have a respectable time of grief or to act as "we should."

Yet, we choose to glorify Him even through this. There are few things in this world that are certain. Unfortunately, one of the most certain is one that we choose to overlook--death. That day, though, will come for all of us until the day our Christ returns. And, until that day, we will live to glorify Him. We will praise Him in all things.

Child of His John 1:12-13

Yet to all who did receive him, to those who believed in his name, he gave the right to become children of God--children born not of natural descent, nor of human decision or a husband's will, but born of God.

She was most definitely a child of His.

Some events bring us face-to-face with reality. I remember teaching VBS (Vacation Bible School) years ago when a parent got very upset because their son had accepted Christ. They only wanted the child to go spend time at the church and enjoy the games and activities. They didn't expect him to come face-to-face with God, and, when he did, it was very unsettling to them. My response was, "Do you not realize that this is real?" Not just an after-school program, not just childcare. We will be teaching your child about the Almighty and he just might believe. It is almost like we need a disclaimer on the invitations.

There were times with Tae when God would remind me I wasn't the one writing her story. In the U.S., I was what some might call "an overprotective parent." We did try to guard her and her heart. (The "overprotective" jury is still out.) However, when we moved here, God seemed to be saying to let her go. That He had her. She was adamant that she was ready. (Back home, she never pushed back, even at the "We will spend three times with any potential boyfriend before a date is even considered" rule. Perhaps this is why she never dated! This one still held true here though!) God showed us that she was ready to go with me into some of the darker places. "There are children there," she would say, "Children that need love." And she was right. She flourished--absolutely flourished.

When her time ended here on this earth, it was another one of those moments. A reality moment. While I knew a lot about Tae, only God knew the day and hour of her departure. Only He had the power to take her from this world and usher her into His presence. As earthly parents, we loved her, oh my goodness, we loved her, but only her Heavenly Father could take her home to the place where she was truly meant to be. What she was truly created for. I think back about her happiness in this world. It was intoxicating. Yet, imagine that same happiness untarnished by sin, by hurt, by evil.

She was reminding us whose she was, and of that she was certain.

He Has Got This Acts 2:25-28

This verse reference that Tae wrote in the journal for Annie over a year ago left me speechless. A year ago, Tae had figured out where she fit in this ministry. She figured out exactly where her spot was. It was with the children. Not just any child but specifically the children who, because of a variety of circumstances, spent their days without any outward pouring of love into their lives. Here is where she thrived.

As you are reading this, remember this was written by an 18-year old girl who was living life to its fullest serving in Nicaragua. She wrote it in a journal to give to her best friend so that she might be encouraged to read her Bible more. Instead, this would be read over a year later, the night when she departed from this world.

David said about him:

"I saw The Lord always before me.
Because he is at my right hand,
I will not be shaken.
Therefore my heart is glad and my tongue rejoices;
my body also will rest in hope,
because you will not abandon me to the realm of the dead,
nor will you let your holy one see decay.
You have made known to me the paths of life;
you will fill me with joy in your presence."

Again, this verse was not in her "top 20" of verses, yet this was included in the journal. In fact, none of those "top 20s" were included; instead, there are verses that reinforce who a child of God is, the purpose and promise that accompanies death on this earth, and how we are to continue. I have been amazed and amazed by God in this whole thing. His fingerprints are all over it. All over it. How can there be any doubt Who is in control? How can we cower when His presence surrounds us?

One Way, Only. Acts 4:12

Salvation is found in no one else, for there is no other name under heaven given to mankind by which we must be saved.

It is what it is.

So not politically correct these days. Especially in America.

I mentioned a while back that it is a good thing God has me in Nicaragua now, because in the US, I'd probably be seen as a raving lunatic.

But it is what it is.

One way, and yet, we've taken that "one way" and turned it into a process of needing to walk forward, say a special prayer or talk only to certain people. I spoke to a guy this week, and his testimony involved simply saying yes as he lay his life and soul in the Father's hands. Yes. And then what?

As I look over the disciples' lives, I don't see them being politically correct over the gospel, with the exception of when Peter denied Christ. Yet we've all tried to put Christ in a box so that we do not offend. But what is so offensive?

In Mark 12:30-31, Christ tells us that the greatest commandments are to "[l]ove the Lord your God with all your heart and with all your soul and with all your mind and with all your strength. The second is this: 'Love your neighbor as yourself.'" What in that is so offensive?

The old hymn says, "They will know we are Christians by our love." Does the world see our love? And not the love that comes from our own hearts, but the love that flows from Christ through us every day?

Praying that the love of Christ overflows out of every believer in this world. Praying that the world will look at this love and say, "I want that. I want that peace, joy and happiness." This is how our Christ will be revealed to the world, through His people allowing His love to flow so freely that those who do condemn can't help but say, "I want to know your God."

One way.

Powerless Romans 8:1-4

Therefore, there is now no condemnation for those who are in Christ Jesus, because through Christ Jesus the law of the Spirit who gives life has set you free from the law of sin and death. For what the law was powerless to do because it was weakened by the flesh, God did by sending his own Son in the likeness of sinful flesh to be a sin offering. And so he condemned sin in the flesh, in order that the righteous requirement of the law might be fully met in us, who do not live according to the flesh but according to the Spirit.

From the time we moved here, we have seen Scripture come to life.

When we do crafts and more ladies come than we have supplies for, there is somehow always enough. When we pass out fruit at the cancer shelter, the fruit seems to multiply. An extra food pack appears at the exact moment we encounter a starving family. Now as I read through and encounter the word *death*, the finality of death takes on new meaning.

When I was reading this for the first time after seeing the journal, the "me" was replaced by Tae's name. It was almost as if she were saying, "Remember the scriptures. I am in Christ, and, through Christ, I have been set free from the law of sin and death. Set free." There are a lot of things that we have accomplished in our world, but when death comes our way, and I mean the finality of death, we are powerless against it.

Powerless.

Trav encountered powerlessness against death when he tried to save our only daughter, but there was no opportunity to save, for her preordained time on this earth had been finished, and he came face to face with that powerlessness. It was the most humbling, gut-wrenching moment in his life. A man so strong, yet so powerless.

Yet, it didn't end there.

That was where our reach ended, but because of Christ and her belonging to Him, she was set free from the sentence of death. I used to despise the sermons ending in, "You never know when your time might come," or, "What if you walk out of here and get into a car accident?" To me, they tried to teach about Christ through fear. But maybe I was wrong. Maybe it wasn't about fear but rather the knowledge and experience of looking the swiftness and finality of death straight on and realizing that (never thought I'd say this) death waits for all of us, and none of us know the day or hour.

When I said goodbye to Tae that day, it was with plans for that evening and the next day. No warning. So where do you stand? Are you certain that when that time comes for you, that you have been set free by the only thing that can set you free from death? Set free by the only thing that has power beyond the reaches of man.

Go and Do Romans 8:31-32

What, then, shall we say in response to these things? If God is for us, who can be against us? He who did not spare his own Son, but gave him up for us all- how will he not also, along with him, graciously give us all things?

As Travis and I were reading through these verses together, the question stood out: "What shall we say in response to this?"

And for us, there is no other response. For Tae, there was no other response. She was all in for God. Period. No what-ifs, no hows, no buts.

I have noticed that when I find myself surrounded by what I now call noise, or when I find myself in a place where I don't see a way, this is when I see God work the greatest. But to get there, I've got to be all in without satan's lies clouding my judgment or clarity. All in, even when the world suggests otherwise. All in, even when circumstances are dire or even tragic.

God's Word is either true or it isn't. So when "noise" comes my way, I go to His word and find what it says. And that's what I hold onto.

Today, go do. Let Christ's love overflow into someone today.

45

No Doubt Hebrews 11:1-3

Now faith is confidence in what we hope for and assurance about what we do not see. This is what the ancients were commended for. By faith we understand that the universe was formed at God's command, so that what is seen was not made out of what was visible.

We serve the same God as Noah, Abraham, Sarah, Isaac, Jacob, Joseph, Moses and David. The same God who parted seas, helped David defeat Goliath, and gave Sarah a son just as He had promised. We serve a big God who has proven Himself time and time again.

Ours is not a generic hope in Christ; it's a certainty that He is who He says He is. He is. And that changes everything. Some days here when it is really hot and dusty, I hope that it will rain, but I have no certainty that it will. Yet, in our Father, I have both the hope which comes with anticipation that His promises will happen, along with the certainty that they will happen. Beyond that, there are very few things (if any) that are truly certain in this world.

We live in a world where we are all guarded so no one takes advantage of us. We put ourselves out there but are always weighing out the other person's agenda against how it will affect ours. One of the best decisions I ever made for my marriage (not that it is always easy) was to assume that Trav always has the best intentions for me, no matter what he says. This took away the ability for satan to manipulate his words and my thoughts. For me, it is the same with God: no matter what happens, what might come our way, He has our back, and I say that with greatest certainty.

God is good.

Only a Shell James 2:26

As the body without the spirit is dead, so faith without deeds is dead.

Each one is more poignant than the one before it, the scripture passages laid out by our daughter over a year prior. Reminding us, pointing towards Christ, then reminding us again of how to continue.

She hadn't danced in years. She was a good dancer. She was the type that could evoke emotion and make you feel the choreography. She did a piece on suicide once that left a full auditorium completely silent, the audience thoughtfully responding to her portrayal of a bullied girl driven to desperation. She stopped dancing in order to, in her own words, devote her whole body to Christ. But I remember this one afternoon, for whatever reason, she started free dancing under the cabana. Just for fun. After that, she started dancing with the ladies at the cancer shelter and kids at the dump. It was her desire to bring arts to the kids she encountered so that they too might learn to express themselves. She was beautiful, and even more so when she danced, because her spirit came alive. This verse became very relevant when she died: "[T]he body without the spirit is dead." Only a shell left behind without the spirit that once filled it. A beautiful shell, but, nonetheless, a shell.

A lot of people have asked how this has changed how I look at life. I think my thoughts can be summed up in the second part of this verse, "[F]aith without deeds is dead." We only have so much time here on this earth, only so much time to do the work that we've been given to do. Each of us. Tae's death has increased the urgency in me to go and do. To go and love. To go and be the hands and feet of Christ. I do not know when my time on earth will end, but what I do know is that until that day comes, I will serve Him to my fullest, and that is the greatest privilege of all.

True Beauty 1 Peter 3:3-4

Your beauty should not come from outward adornment, such as elaborate hairstyles and the wearing of gold jewelry or fine clothes. Rather, it should be that of your inner self, the unfading beauty of a gentle and quiet spirit, which is of great worth in God's sight.

We hear it said over and over that beauty is only skin deep, and true beauty is what is found on the inside. Unfortunately, this saying has become a cliché, and the truth has been lost.

Tae had her own sense of style. She loved to take old clothes, tear them apart and sew them back together into something new, and, somehow, someway, she could pull it off. Looking back, I think that came from who she was inside. She was confident in Whose she was, and that was beautiful.

We saw her transform from a very strong-willed child into a fearless young woman. That transformation was made through Christ. Totally sold out, here I am, use me however you want. Every single day. She picked up lice from the village children so many times that lice treatment because a weekly routine. She never flinched or shied away from where He was leading her. She never denied a dirty child the hug he needed.

So many people asked us how our teenage daughter was doing down here. She flourished in a way that only God's spirit could have enabled.

God isn't telling us not to be beautiful here. He's telling us not to find our beauty in worldly adornments but to let His beauty shine through our lives.

Go shine today.

True Purpose 1 Peter 1:1-4

To God's elect, exiles scattered through the provinces of Pontus, Galatia, Cappadocia, Asia and Bithynia, who have been chosen according to the foreknowledge of God the Father, through the sanctifying work of the Spirit, to be obedient to Jesus Christ and sprinkled with his blood: Grace and peace be yours in abundance. Praise be to the God and Father of our Lord Jesus Christ! In his great mercy he has given us new birth into a living hope through the resurrection of Jesus Christ from the dead, and into an inheritance that can never perish, spoil or fade. This inheritance is kept in heaven for you."

Looking back, it doesn't surprise me that Tae would write down I Peter in her journal for Annie with the word *hope* interwoven throughout its tapestry of words. *Hope.*

There came a time before we moved here when we realized we would not be able to save the world. That no matter how much work we do in the village, the food we distribute, the feet we are able to put shoes on, the houses we build, the wells we drill, the gardens we plant, we will not fix this. Jesus told us that we will always have poverty, so even our endless efforts will not resolve the economic situation of the globe, or even our small section of it.

Why, then, should we do this work? Our purpose is to share Christ's love by doing each of those actions and by building relationships. When they ask why we are working, we can share the hope that can only be found in Christ, which is a hope that doesn't tarnish, fade, spoil or perish. Eternal hope.

And that is why we are here. Obedience doesn't come easy. The world will tell you that you are crazy. Fellow Christians may tell you that you've suffered too much already, but obedience to Jesus Christ comes with a price. The letting-go of things of this world, the believing that His word holds true in every circumstance, the courage to stand when all others step aside: these are only some of the costs.

Belief for us tends to be easy sometimes. It even comes with perks like affiliation with the popular church in our town or networking opportunities in our denomination. But there are Christians around the world today that are burned alive for their faith. Would your faith stand when encountering blazing fire? Would mine? And since we aren't encountering blazing fire, what are we doing with the freedom of expression that we have been given? Are we bold?

Eternal hope. That's the prize.

Force Field 1 Peter 1:5-7

[W]ho through faith are shielded by God's power until the coming of the salvation that is ready to be revealed in the last time. In all this you greatly rejoice, though now for a little while you may have had to suffer grief in all kinds of trials. These have come so that the proven genuineness of your faith--of greater worth than gold, which perishes even though refined by fire--may result in praise, glory and honor when Jesus Christ is revealed.

About a year ago, Slaton was playing with some friends close enough to be in earshot. Trav and I heard him tell the boy he was playing with (who was older and bigger) to take his best shot. He proceeded to explain that he had his force field on, so he couldn't be hurt. As we watched, the boy clarified twice with Slate, and each time he was confident that he couldn't be hurt. He stood tall as the other boy hit him in the stomach as hard as he could. Slate took a deep breath and walked away. As I came to his side, I could hear him talking to himself. He really thought he had a force shield that could not be penetrated just like the Power Rangers.

Through faith, we are shielded by God's power. This doesn't mean that we won't experience hardships; in fact, Peter indicates these trials are part of our refining process, and our faith will be made stronger for it. Yet, our souls cannot be harmed, touched or challenged once we have salvation in Jesus Christ. Can't be.

I think we often just skim the surface of our world. Our perspective starts to take on very worldly overtones, shallow and skewed. It is when we face true hardships that we stop and take an account of what matters, and we see how quickly the impurities of our lives rise to the surface, and are skimmed away many times without our knowledge.

51

I can tell you exactly what I was worried about before I got the phone call about Tae. I was on my way to pick up the attorney to perform a double wedding in the dump. I was concerned about whether or not the right paperwork would be there, whether or not I had bought enough cake and whether or not it would rain. They were all valid concerns, but the souls of those present at the wedding were not one of my concerns.

I was caught up in the busyness of what we were doing that day. I know, details are important, and it is all part of the mission of what we are doing, so maybe their souls were a given. But I am convinced a focus on the everyday things is one of the very ploys satan uses to distract us.

We don't consider Tae's death a trial. We are all going to die. We just are. We look at Tae's death as a job well-finished and her relocating to heaven. The trial comes in our response to her absence in this world. The trial comes in carrying on or allowing satan to rob us of finishing our race well. The trial comes in allowing the impurities to be skimmed off or fighting to hold on to them, because to let them go would change our lives.

And the prize is the greatest freedom imaginable.

Our Choice 1 Peter 1:8-9

Though you have not seen him, you love him; and even though you do not see him now, you believe in him and are filled with an inexpressible and glorious joy, for you are receiving the end result of your faith, the salvation of your souls.

Inexpressible and glorious joy.

There is a peace that comes from knowing, really knowing, Whose you are. Through that confidence comes freedom, and through that freedom, joy simply overflows. As we walk this path of faith, we find moments in our day-to-day lives when we have the opportunity to practice obedience and discipline. Maybe it is choosing not to gossip at work, maybe it is choosing to extend grace to the driver who is driving too slow or cuts you off, maybe it is choosing to demonstrate unconditional love to your family, the ones who experience your life behind closed doors, or maybe it is choosing to give back the extra change you were mistakenly given at the store.

Each one of these requires action on our part. How do we choose to respond? The other parties can stomp on our lives and create the biggest chaos, but when our turn comes, how do we respond? Over time, as we choose to respond as Christ would respond, we find that our souls are filled with uncontainable joy. We were created for good. We were. One choice put sin in this world, and every choice either puts sin in our lives or pushes it away. Several years ago the idea of WWJD came out. What Would Jesus Do? And that's it. What would He do? I can tell you that hate inside your mind and soul grows, and its flame is fanned by satan.

And I know, "but he," "but she," "but they." I know. But the only person I can control is me. My thoughts, my actions. When we stand before Christ, we stand alone. Alone. No excuses and no jury trial. Have we taken the gifts we have been given and used them for His kingdom and for others' souls? Have we taken the free will we have been given and used it to exercise mercy and grace so that others might see Christ through us?

I say over and over again that what I miss most in Tae is serving beside her. And friends, it wasn't just our scheduled ministry times, it was anywhere she saw an opportunity to extend love. Her God wasn't in a box to pull out at our ministry stops or on Sunday. He was full-on all the time. Life is too short. Way too short to live miserable, stressed, hateful, jaded, disappointed and depressed. Too short to waste another day, another moment or another breath.

Starting today, choose Christ. Choose joy. Choose to respond out of love even while tears flow down your face. Live as we were created to be.

Own Your Faith 1 Peter 1:10-12

Concerning this salvation, the prophets, who spoke of the grace that was to come to you, searched intently and with the greatest care, trying to find out the time and circumstances to which the Spirit of Christ in them was pointing when he predicted the sufferings of the Messiah and the glories that would follow. It was revealed to them that they were not serving themselves but you, when they spoke of the things that have now been told you by those who have preached the gospel to you by the Holy Spirit sent from heaven. Even angels long to look into these things.

"They searched intently and with the greatest care." Oh Lord, I pray that when I study Your word, I would search intently and with greatest care. I pray that my discernment would be sharpened and that the gravity of the Truth would never fail to pierce my heart. Too many times, I have read quickly through Your Truth without searching or have listened without the reverence of those who came before us.

I remember one time specifically seeking God's Truth several years before I finally accepted Christ. I asked a friend specific questions about her Christ, to which she had no response other than it was better to believe and it not be true than to not believe and burn in hell. I have a difficult time accepting that logic. I just do. During what I call my "actively seeking phase," I would ask the same questions to those who would come to our house representing different religions, and they knew the answers. They could quickly turn in their literature and show me step-by-step. I found this to be true time and time again.

Today, we serve in some relatively dangerous areas, areas I would not go into if I didn't have a relationship with those we are going to serve. Daily, I meet people with other beliefs boldly encountering the danger. Walking at nighttime, they bring their beliefs to those who will listen. We have the greatest Power of all behind us, but we are cautious to the point of not engaging.

55

Satan has encouraged us to fill our lives with things and events we "need." He has encouraged us to fill our homes with Bibles that are rarely opened, much less searched intently and with greatest care. With this comes the loss of intimately knowing Our Father, of weaving into our hearts the Truth that will truly set us free. The world may call us Christians because we go to church, carry a Bible, walked down an aisle, or give to the poor, but the world doesn't get to decide. In fact, the world will placate our souls into believing that we are solid when we really know that we are not. This is not a game based on attendance, and there literally is not a second place. With these high stakes, how can we keep from pouring God's words into our hearts? Searching intently and carefully so that we might be called a Christian by the only Voice that matters.

Prepare 1 Peter 1:13-16

Therefore, with minds that are alert and fully sober, set your hope fully on the grace to be brought to you when Jesus Christ is revealed at his coming. As obedient children, do not conform to the evil desires you had when you lived in ignorance. But just as he who called you is holy, so be holy in all you do; for it is written: "Be holy because I am holy."

Prepare your mind for action. Be self-controlled. Set your hope on the grace to be brought to you.

I'm reminded time and time again that this is not a passive part of our world. When we read Job, we are given an insight into satan traversing across this earth. Our earth, going back and forth in it. Our world. So even when I choose not to engage, the game goes on. With me or without me. By not engaging I don't take myself out of play; instead, I take away my best defenses.

Prepare my mind for action. What goes in my mind? What thoughts do I allow to linger? Do I have God's words so embedded in who I am that they quickly come to mind when I need a defense?

Be self-controlled. Does what I say and do bring glory to our Father, or does it give me relief for a fleeting moment of time? Does it draw people to Him or push them away? This is not about me. It is about serving others so that He might be known.

Hope. Where is my hope really found? Is it the gift of hope from Christ or is it "hope" that I create as I pseudo-control my world and those around me?

We are told to be holy just as He is. Holy. Do we know what that means? Holy in some places means something totally different from others. Would we recognize holy if we saw it, even if it were different than us? I find my definition of holy in these verses. Christ is our example. Be Christ-like. Love deeply. Be self-controlled. Key word here is "self." We cannot control others. We can't.

We might bend them with force or bruise them with our words, but we will never control their souls. If we do as Christ did, and be a humble example, sure of who we are, Christ will be glorified.

When Christ came, He didn't come to judge. He came to be a holy example to us all. All of us. He was touchable to all. Each and every one. Somehow we have gotten to a point in our world where we are almost afraid to love, because to love means that we agree with whatever the person does. Love in spite of. Love on them, let them see Jesus through you. Don't worry about being affiliated with the wrong group. Jesus will take them just as he has taken all of his obedient followers and will transform them just as he took us and is constantly transforming us. We just have to be the light. Not the judge and jury. Just the light.

Reverent Fear 1 Peter 1:17

Since you call on a Father who judges each person's work impartially, live out your time as foreigners here in reverent fear.

Reverent fear. Not just fear but reverent fear.

Deepest respect. Eternal honor. We are told in this verse to live our lives as foreigners here in reverent fear. Do you feel like you fit in this world? If the world were like high school, would you be sitting at the "popular table?"

We aren't supposed to "fit" here. We aren't. This world as it is will never be our home. There are too many evil forces at play, creating constant discomfort to our souls. We were created to be surrounded by holiness. That is the true desire of our inner being, yet we try so hard to find comfort here. We try so hard to fit in here. But what do we gain? A few years of bought happiness? A weekend of pleasure followed by a full week of suffering hanging on until the next weekend so we can make ourselves feel better again? As Christians, we will not find our place in this world. We will not. The sooner we accept we will always be strangers in this world, the sooner we will stop serving this world and start fully serving our Father. We will start searching for a place in this world we can serve to further *His* kingdom, not ours. We will start living a life of obedience and discipline instead of wasting time trying to fit pieces of two different puzzles together.

We will start living in reverent fear of God.

In this, we will find joy. True joy that will withstand the greatest trials and challenges we will face. Not the "joy" that disappears as soon as we partake of its substance, but joy that is interwoven into our hearts. That joy. The joy that overcomes when you lose your job and the people you thought were your friends. The joy that reminds you "we battle not against flesh and blood" when your marriage falls apart. That joy. The joy that is revealed when you bury your only daughter, and you realize the evil in this world will never be able to hurt her again. That joy. And this is eternal joy. Not joy that is fleeting or that will eventually turn into bondage, but eternal joy.

Tae never fit into this world. She was created different from this world, just as we all were, and she chose at an early age to embrace that difference and to use it for her God. It was a choice just as it is for us. How do we choose to live every day? Do we succumb to the trappings of a world that is fleeting, or do we put our hope in eternity? I love the song, "What Do I Know of Holy?" I love the words. They speak to my soul. Reverent fear. Is He fire? Is He fury? Is He beautiful? What do I know of Holy?

I'm afraid that if we truly knew Holy, our lives would be drastically different. We would live as we were born to live, with reverent fear.

Only Plan A 1 Peter 1:18-21

For you know that it was not with perishable things such as silver or gold that you were redeemed from the empty way of life handed down to you from your ancestors, but with the precious blood of Christ, a lamb without blemish or defect. He was chosen before the creation of the world, but was revealed in these last times for your sake. Through him you believe in God, who raised him from the dead and glorified him, and so your faith and hope are in God.

He was chosen before the creation of the world. Chosen before sin entered this world. Chosen before we were even born. Chosen before Tae died.

Christ being chosen to die wasn't "Plan B." It wasn't God's way of trying to fix things after everything spiraled out of His control; it was part of the plan from the very beginning.

And in this, we can find solid faith and hope. Solid. Not ebbing and flowing with the changes of the ocean's tides. Not fading in and out with the alignment of the stars. But solid and firm faith and hope. Constant.

The world knows that we need this. It is evident by the wares we are enticed to buy and by the ploys by which we are entrapped. Psychics, horoscopes, tarot cards. We are searching for someone, any person or thing that can give us something "firm" to cling to. We ask for answers to our future. The answer is simply to place your hope and faith in God.

From the moment I received the phone call that would change our lives as we knew it, I knew beyond a doubt that God knew the path beforehand. Not just the path I would walk, but the path that everyone touched by the news that day would trudge along. And I knew from the deepest part of my soul, that my God was a God who is just, powerful, almighty, loving, all-knowing and constant. I didn't have to worry about where He would stand or what His response would be because I knew who He was. He is a rock upon which I have built my house. The firmest of all foundations.

I love the show *Survivor* for the sheer fun of people-watching. I have always said the only way I would play the game is if I knew for sure I had one person who had my back. No matter what. No matter what I said or did. No matter the cost or gain. My back, always. We think there are people we love who have our back no matter what. Or we have enough money or power or possessions that we have our own back. But in this world, there is only One we can count on. Only One, and that is Christ.

So I continue "playing" this game of Survivor in this world, knowing that the One who is the most reliable of all is my ally. My Christ.

Be strong today. The game we play is real.

Stop 1 Peter 2:1

Therefore, rid yourselves of all malice and all deceit, hypocrisy, envy, and slander of every kind.

Lice is an everyday reality in our world. Tae had lice so often we would laugh about her weekly "beauty" treatments. We figured no matter how dirty the conditions are, no matter how dirty we might get, our bodies can always be washed. This is a small price to pay to extend love by touch.

Ridding ourselves of the filth Peter speaks of is not as easy as washing with lice treatment and body wash. Malice and all deceit, hypocrisy, envy, and slander of every kind. We are instructed to rid ourselves of them, simply get them out of our lives. We are to do it ourselves. Not rid someone else's life of all malice and deceit, hypocrisy, envy, and slander of every kind, but my own life, and not just some, but all. Not just the worst kinds, but all.

This is difficult, but the freedom gained in not allowing satan to have any part in our world is ours to have. When we choose to keep malice, deceit, hypocrisy, envy and slander in our lives, even when the world says we are justified in doing so, we are allowing satan to work through us, not Christ. It goes deeper than simply hurting someone's feelings or getting back at them or standing up for ourselves. It does. There are only two teams playing this game of life, so to speak. Which team do our actions portray?

So how do we stop? How do we break cycles that have been in play for generations? We live differently. We choose to do the opposite of what has been done to us. Instead of a hateful glare back, try a smile, or if you can't do that, walk away before you perpetuate the bad. Instead of gossiping or listening to the gossip, use this time to build the person up. Building them up doesn't make you look smaller; it breaks the cycle.

Our true colors show the brightest to those who see us behind closed doors. I can feed the poor all day, but if I don't have that same compassion for my family, then what I've just done is for naught.

If I don't treat my husband with respect and love in our home, my children will learn that God's Word is only to be followed when others see. Tae was part of the refining fire God used to help me rid my life of many things, and to remind me when my actions at home didn't exemplify Christ.

Our inner circle must be filled with people who will not only encourage us, but will also speak truth into our lives. I once had one of my inner circle point out to me that the person I was outside of my workplace was not the same person I portrayed inside. Did I lead out of kindness and encouragement, or did I lead by intimidation? Did I lead differently from the world? This was a hard one to take, but she spoke truth and it changed my life.

Pray today that God would point out any areas of malice, deceit, slander, hypocrisy or envy.

Choose different actions today.

Preparing for the Journey 1 Peter 2:2-3

Like newborn babies, crave pure spiritual milk, so that by it you may grow up in your salvation, now that you have tasted that the Lord is good.

David and Goliath, Jesus walking on water, the walls of Jericho falling, Daniel and the lion's den.

Incredible history of God's provision and protection of His people. The beginning "milk" of the Bible. The children's stories. The idea is that through these examples we might taste the goodness of the Lord and then crave more. We might crave to go deeper and hunger to mature in our faith.

Unfortunately, many times we linger where we feel most comfortable. We stay where we know how the story ends, and it always ends well. But God calls us to grow up. To stop thinking as a child, to stop giving in to how we feel, to stop being impulsive, and to be obedient to Him. Go deeper.

As parents, we need to be sure we are encouraging our children in their spiritual journey. I'm afraid we spend more time developing their talents in sports and other interests than we do their spiritual journey. I can tell you, as a mother who recently looked upon the dead body of her only daughter, I wasn't thankful for the thousands of hours of gymnastics lessons or dance, but for the spiritual journey that I knew she had. Again, the world lulls us into believing that to develop our children, we must conform them to the world and its challenges. We must prepare them specifically for the world they live in. While I believe that in part this is true, the difference comes in how we prepare them. Do we focus on God? Do we really know where our children stand? Are we depending on others to mentor the children God gave to us? Youth pastors and teachers are great, but our children and their eternal salvation are ours, as parents, alone to foster, encourage and grow. Sounds radically different from our world, doesn't it? Isn't this the life we were called to live?

It may mean not attending games or practices on Sundays so our families can worship together, it may mean not competing in certain competitions because the dances are inspired by strip clubs, it may mean we don't have cable or block certain channels. I used to think that in order to prepare my children for this world, I couldn't shelter them. God has since shown me that my part in preparation was showing them a life to live that was set apart. He assured me that it was okay to go against the grain and that sometimes we had to stand up and say, "No, we will not be doing that. I'm sorry about what the cost might be, but your relationship to our Father is worth far more."

Let's enjoy our children. Play with them, love on them, encourage and guide them, but let's be sure the areas we stress in their lives reflect the true priorities of our hearts. We say "God first" but do we live God-first in our families? Or, have we only been lapping milk?

Factions that Fail Us 1 Peter 2:4-6

As you come to Him, the living Stone--rejected by humans but chosen by God and precious to Him--you also, like living stones, are being built into a spiritual house to be a holy priesthood, offering spiritual sacrifices acceptable to God through Jesus Christ. For in Scripture it says: "See, I lay a stone in Zion, a chosen and precious cornerstone, and the one who trusts in him will never be put to shame."

From the moment word traveled about Tae's time on this earth ending, we saw Christ's Church in action. From rushing to be by our side to sending literally hundreds of messages, God's people responded with such magnitude that we were completely surrounded by Truth. We prayed that God would build a hedge of protection around us, and, on that day, in that hour, He built a hedge made of His people that was impenetrable. People from different churches and even different nations came and surrounded us. It didn't matter. They were God's people. He told them to act, and they responded.

We've created such vast differences in our churches. We have broken ourselves up into so many factions that, I'm afraid, instead of being appealing to a broken world, we've confused the gospel message. In John 14:6, Christ is very clear: "I am the way and the truth and the life. No one comes to the Father except through me." Yet, we've created so many different denominations that separate us. Satan has caused confusion and blurred lines when there is black and white.

Christ is the cornerstone, and we are simply stones laid amongst other believers. I don't believe the stones are separated by denominations. Baptist on this wall, Church of Christ on that wall, Lutherans over here, and on and on. There is only one cornerstone. Only one. This is not a manmade church; it is God-ordained. God made.

I love when people ask about Project H.O.P.E.'s denominational affiliation. A board of directors and a staff that is multidenominational and from different nations governs it.

And the next statement that typically follows is, "That must be difficult." But it isn't. The main thing is the main thing. Period. We share the common belief that there is one way. Christ. Our differences in Biblical interpretation never override that, and I think that is powerful. We must be careful that we don't divide our house against itself because when we do, when we divide ourselves as believers, we make ourselves ineffective.

When God calls His church to action, we must be ready to respond. We must be solidly aligned with His cornerstone. What an honor we have been given to be used in His spiritual house. May we be found worthy of it.

I Once was Blind 1 Peter 2:7-8

Now to you who believe, this stone is precious. But to those who do not believe, "The stone the builders rejected has become the cornerstone," and, "A stone that causes people to stumble and a rock that makes them fall." They stumble because they disobey the message--which is also what they were destined for.

I stumbled and fell over this stone as a young person; in fact, I thought it was the craziest brainwashing scheme ever. I grew up going to church. I vividly remember Sunday school lessons and sermons, but I never "bought into" any of it. Once I graduated high school and went to college, I quickly tossed aside any thoughts of God. I was never a partier or huge risk taker (Looking back, God was protecting me even then.). It wasn't until our son, Devon, decided that he wanted to go to church just like his friends did, that church came back into my world. Even though I desperately tried to talk him out of it (yes, I did), he was persistent, and we finally gave in.

And a battle began. In my quest for Truth, I explored other religions. I was still unable to accept the Truth from my youth, but I took that first step of walking into a church again and being open to the possibility of the Gospel being true. After that, God gave me an unquenchable desire for His word. Satan threw at me every question or concern I had ever had concerning God. God placed people in our world who were real in their faith, and satan reminded me of every hypocrite I'd ever met until I finally came to the place where my "eyes" were opened. I just knew. I can't quite explain it, but the floodgates opened and I could "see" Truth, and in my heart, I could reconcile faith, God and Jesus Christ without question.

I was in my late 20s and literally had to go back to people whose faith I had discouraged and apologize and thank them for their witness. I realized that I was very prideful in my stance against the trappings of religion. Satan used my desire for autonomy and quest for pure facts to place a wedge between myself and the only One who could truly set me free. A wedge that until I saw if for what it was, condemned my soul.

I can relate to Saul/Paul in the Bible. Totally sold out. A Damascus Road experience, first being sold out against Christ because he thought he was doing the right thing and then having a moment of reckoning and realizing that everything he had been fighting against was really the Truth all along. I get that.

I wasn't always a believer. I remember what it was like living without a Savior. I remember being my own and living apart from my Creator. I have often been told that my excitement or zealousness for Christ will eventually wane, but I find the more I seek Him and the more He is revealed to me, the more excited I become. I spent too many years apart from Him living in a world of darkness that masqueraded itself as light. I am beyond humbled to take His light into the darkness revealing it for what it is: lies, deceit and destruction. Let's not stumble or fall anymore but rather be willing living stones.

Chosen 1 Peter 2:9-10

But you are a chosen people, a royal priesthood, a holy nation, God's special possession, that you may declare the praises of him who called you out of darkness into his wonderful light. Once you were not a people, but now you are the people of God, once you had not received mercy, but now you have received mercy.

I'm afraid that we have become a people that feeds off of adrenaline and then we respond. We follow the headlines in the news and we respond. Getting close to summer? We try to get into shape. New Year's Day coming? We vow to keep our resolutions this time. New Bible devotion? This one we will finish. We lost our temper again? This time we will change. Someone we know dies? We will hold our children tighter and live in the moment. Until we don't.

We get caught up in a world that tries to possess our whole being every moment, every day, so much so that we forget the most important part. We are the people of God. We are His people. Those who know Him and believe in Him are His people. Every day. Every hour.

With this comes great promises. He will never leave us, never forsake us. Never. Following this world, we will have eternal salvation and these are great promises.

Hold onto each and every one of them. Every day. Did you wake up today remembering Whose you are? That you have been called by the Lord Most High? Or was that the furthest thing from your mind?

This life isn't about doing church. This is about living worthy of the One to Whom we belong, every day, every moment. When we first moved down here, I prayed that God would let me see as He sees. About four months ago, that prayer changed to, "Let me learn to give praise and find joy in all circumstances." That prayer did not bring about Tae's death, but living through her death will help mold us into a more Christ-like image.

Her death has broken us, and He is mending our hearts with His Truth, His love. Her death has brought sorrow deeper than we've never experienced before, but in that sorrow, He has given us joy. Her death has brought us face to face with evil in a place I've never been before, but amidst that evil, I've experienced His protection as never before. Her death should have left us lonely, but He sent His people, our people, to surround us.

Remember, as a child of God, we are His. It has nothing to do with our earthy accomplishments. Nothing. Don't place your value or identity on anything other than being a child of His. Then live so others might know Him.

Foreign Always 1 Peter 2:11-12

Dear friends, I urge you, as foreigners and exiles, to abstain from sinful desires, which wage war against your soul. Live such good lives among pagans that, though they accuse you of doing wrong, they may see your good deeds and glorify God on the day he visits us.

Live in such a way that we bring glory and honor to our Creator. Every day in every circumstance. This will be foreign to this world.

The book of I Peter tells us how we are to live so that others might know Him. We are taught how we are to respond and how we should carry ourselves. Because of whose we are, we are to choose to be different in order to glorify our Father.

When we are betrayed, ridiculed, slandered or worse, our response is the only thing we can control. God tells us to live such good lives that our critics will take notice and will glorify God. The world we live in tells us we must stand up for ourselves or we will lose all respect, that we must defend our honor, we must defend our character. But this has never been about us. We are to glorify Him, not ourselves. Not our honor, not our character, but His. He will be glorified in our responses, or not.

The battle that rages against souls tries to poke and prod us, looking for weakness in our armor. Is it our pride that is weak? Is it our feelings? What can satan provoke within us that will cause us to choose to respond in a manner that reflects this world and not our Heavenly Father?

If we can choose to respond differently to this evil and respond as children of God, then there will be a pause in the interaction. The fire of destruction will be weakened as we choose not to add fuel to a fire started by satan. I believe when we can see it isn't flesh and blood we battle against, but rather the evil of this world, we start shining light in a dark world.

I know that Jesus was angry in the temple, but what caused His anger? Defilement of His Father's house caused Him to react forcefully. People who were supposed to be taking care of His Father's people were actually taking advantage of them, and this brought out the wrath of Christ. Jesus was provoked beyond our imagination, betrayed at the greatest level, mocked, slandered, and, yet, He did not allow satan to provoke a worldly response. Maybe if He would have, the world would have accepted Him better: "Oh, wait, he is one of us." But no, it was never about Christ either, but the One who sent Him.

We can choose to respond however we wish, and we will find those in this world who will praise our actions. It is your choice. But for those who are children of Our Father, we have been called to live as strangers to this world. We have been called to glorify our Father with our actions. All of them.

Without Commentary 1 Peter 2:13-15

Submit yourselves for the Lord's sake to every human authority: whether to the emperor, as the supreme authority, or to governors, who are sent by him to punish those who do wrong and to commend those who do right. For it is God's will that by doing good you should silence the ignorant talk of foolish people.

As Christians, as children of God, we are to be model citizens, not only following the laws of our government, but also using our words to support those who govern us. God isn't surprised by anything; therefore, those in authority have been placed there by His consent. We are to obey the laws of our land without commentary. By doing this, doing good, we can silence the words of those who are foolish.

I have learned that it is so much more effective to disagree with someone and respectfully work alongside them, supporting the common cause and refraining from judgment. In my younger days, I felt it was more about principle. I wanted to know where each person stood so I could judge them. That wasn't Christ-like at all. Everyone that you encounter should know Whose you are and where you stand without you saying a word. By your actions, by your chosen responses, they should know, and you will either silence ignorant talk or you will be part of that ignorant talk.

Christ walked among many different kinds of people. He was under the authority of rulers who were not believers, yet there was never a question as to His ultimate authority. By His actions, every day, everyone knew.

We are under the rule and authority of those that are not believers. My family is under the authority and rulings of those that, well, let's just say are not followers. Yet, to raise words against them, to refuse to follow their authority, would cause us to lose our ability to be effective missionaries in this country. Be respectful, be the peacemakers and live in such a way that even those who criticize us as children of God, in their time of need will seek us out asking for prayer to our Father. Will they seek and ask if they know beforehand that they will have to walk through hatred? No, but if they know they will encounter love and respect for their held position, they will seek us out and then they will listen.

75

There is no question that we serve God first. No surprise that He is our ultimate authority, but He has called us to choose to live in such a way that we draw others to Him. Not all of our leaders will be Christian. We will probably come to a place in history where Christians will be in the minority. Some of our sisters and brothers already live like this. So how are we to respond? According to our early scriptures, we are to rid ourselves of all malice, deceit, hypocrisy, envy and slander. All. This includes our elected and appointed officials. Be the peacemakers.

Freedom 1 Peter 2:16-17

Live as free people, but do not use your freedom as a cover-up for evil; live as God's slaves. Show proper respect to everyone, love the family of believers, fear God, honor the emperor.

There is freedom found in Christ. True freedom. Many people will look at Christianity and see rules, dos and don'ts. Judgment. But they have been blinded to the Truth.

Christ's word is constant: today, tomorrow, the same. While I am being tempted, when I fall into temptation and sin, and when I repent, He does not change. It was, it is, it will forever be. However, this world is not. Satan is not. When we are being tempted by satan, he will masquerade as light, as goodness, as freedom. When we succumb to sin, when we act and it brings shame to our Creator, satan rejoices for himself, but as for us, he condemns us, he ridicules, he reminds us how weak we are, how unworthy, how disappointing we must be. His words are not constant. They aren't truth and they will change however they need to in order to bring sin upon this world. Passive aggressive at its finest.

I have seen the destruction of abortion many times. We all know where God stands on the issue. But satan will tell you that it is your body, your right and your freedom. Until the moment that it is too late, and in the dark of the night, he condemns and his message changes. Time and time again, I've held women in my arms crying because of the lies that cost their children's lives, and the people and friends who initially supported them in their "rightful" decision are gone, and they are alone.

The same with prostitution, affairs, "having it all." And the list goes on and on.

So when we completely turn our lives over to Christ and become a willing vessel for Him to fill, we start living in Truth. We begin to live on a foundation that is secure. The message is what it is, no matter what our response has been. It does not change.

And in this, we find the greatest freedom. No longer are we shackled by the bondages of this world, where lies try to entrap us; rather, we live according to our Father's desires, which is how we were created to live.

An Example 1 Peter 2:18-21

Slaves, in reverent fear of God submit yourselves to your masters, not only to those who are good and considerate, but also to those who are harsh. For it is commendable if someone bears up under the pain of unjust suffering because they are conscious of God. But how is it to your credit if you receive a beating for doing wrong and endure it? But if you suffer for doing good and you endure it, this is commendable before God. To this you were called, because Christ suffered for you, leaving you an example, that you should follow in his steps.

Christ left us an example.

It is a joke around my house that before I embark on any new activity or experience, I read everything I can find on the topic. I have owned so many self-help books it is almost embarrassing. Good books. Recommended books. Books off the *New York Times* best seller list. Several years ago, I decided to train for an adventure race and needed to start running for the first time. I read for two months before I ever laced up my running shoes.

I have done the same thing with my walk in faith. I have read books on how to pray, how to be a better Christian wife, how to raise my children, how to have a better Christian marriage. Praying for the "10 practical steps" that I can do in order to do this right. Give me a checklist. I would meet godly people and either try to emulate their lives or try to figure out what they did that made them different in this journey with Christ.

And one day, God led me again to the story about the rich young ruler and I saw it in a different light. Here was a man who truly wanted to follow Christ, had followed the "list" and yet still wasn't quite there and he knew it. He knew it. Just as we know when we aren't where we are to be. And he asked Jesus what he must do to inherit eternal life. I had always focused on him not being able to give up his riches to follow Christ and missed what came before. He knew and had obeyed all of the commandments that Christ listed, and he still only called Jesus "Good Teacher," not Lord, not Savior. In spite of following the rules and practical advice, he still was not a follower of Christ.

So what was it that he was missing? It wasn't only because he was wealthy because other wealthy people didn't have to give up their riches.

What God showed me that day was that it wasn't about a list, a method, a best way, it was about an only way. Him. Christ is our example. He is the One we follow. Books are great and I LOVE to read, but we need to be sure it is Him we are seeking and not just seeking. I tell my students who are studying for tests not to spend so much time preparing to study and organizing what they are going to study that they run out of time for studying for the test itself! Let's be careful not to spend too much of our time preparing, organizing and trying to find the perfect devotional or Bible, and miss having a relationship with Him.

It is Jesus. Quite simple. We try to make it harder than it is. He is the example. Not your pastor, not your mentor, not me, not Taellor. To try to emulate others' lives would result in trying to live a life planned by God but a life that is not your own. Seek Christ. Follow Him and be prepared to experience a life that is literally not of this world.

Suffering Gracefully 1 Peter 2:22-23

"He committed no sin, and no deceit was found in his mouth."

When they hurled their insults at Him, He did not retaliate; when He suffered, He made no threats. Instead, He trusted Himself to He who judges justly.

How do you face suffering? As children of God, we may face suffering because of consequences of our own actions or simply because we are living in a fallen world. Christ lived His life here without sin. Therefore, all of the suffering that was brought upon Him was the result of a fallen world. He left us the greatest example of how to suffer, especially during times when it isn't our fault.

We need to justify ourselves. From the time we are kids on the playground, insults are hurled freely back and forth to clarify who we really are. Lies are spread that ruin reputations, deceit regarding well-lived lives starts to take root and satan has succeeded in creating havoc. Havoc does not lend itself to the nurturing of our souls but the destruction of those around us.

Jesus has left us a living example of facing suffering with patience, compassion and confidence knowing full well Who is in control. He knew and trusted the One who held His future. God. So when suffering came His way, He didn't try to talk His way out of it. He didn't meet their accusations with equal hatred. He didn't call down a legion of angels to save Him. He walked in obedience.

Not everyone will like us. In fact, most probably will not. Live a life set apart from this world and you will suffer for His name. You will. Choose to make decisions that glorify Him and you will find that the world will distance itself from you. For some, that's a scary thing. But realize, as you are being treated differently, as lies are being hurled your way, as you choose to walk a different path, they will be watching. They will watch your reaction just as they watched Jesus. And what they see from you will either push them toward Christ or will assist satan in pulling them away.

Tae's death has been the most difficult circumstance on this earth we have had to face. When we lost Tae, I imagined Mary, Jesus' mother, I imagined Abraham instructed to take Isaac to the mountain as a sacrifice, I imagined Job as all of his boys and girls were gone in an instant. For the first time, I knew, really knew, their pain. I could feel it. The breathlessness of suddenness, the heartbreak of finality, the emptiness of a parent's arms, and yet, there was something else, the thing that empowers the ability to carry on. Obedience in knowing at the core of my being Who was really in charge. Their faith was unmovable, unwavering, more than words in a song they had sung. Their faith was a faith that was interwoven into their very being.

We must strive daily to have that faith. I believe it is achieved by continual daily communion with our Father just like Abraham, Moses, Noah, Sarah. Jesus. Scheduled quiet times are wonderful, but I believe the intent is that they are to be carried on into the rest of your day. You don't have to "go before the Father" when you've been walking and talking with Him all day. So when insults, slander, deceit, lies and hurt feelings come our way, we have been continually bathed in His thoughts and His desires, and we respond in a manner that glorifies our Father instead of the fleeting satisfaction of knowing that we got the last word.

Today, talk to Him as you go about your day. It may seem strange at first, but it will become second nature. Sometimes we live our lives thinking He is so far away, when really it is we who have chosen not to include Him in our every moment. He won't push Himself on you. He's already there.

Our Overseer 1 Peter 2:24-25

"He himself bore our sins" in his body on the cross, so that we might die to sins and live for righteousness; "by his wounds you have been healed." For "you were like sheep going astray," but now you have returned to the Shepherd and Overseer of your souls.

The Overseer of my soul. He's our Comforter, the Great I Am, my Protector, my Shield, the Great Physician, the Way, the Truth and the Life, and the list could go on and on. The Overseer of my soul.

As we make our way through today, let us pause and reflect on the Overseer of our souls. Whatever happens in the here and now, whether I encounter trials, pain or success, I can rest assured that my soul is guarded and protected by the Almighty.

My mother gave me a special diamond ring when Taellor was born. A beautiful ring that I wore constantly until the day when the stone fell out of the setting. Distraught, Travis and I looked for hours in the place where I had lost it until I finally came to realize that it was forever lost to me. About four months later, Mom was diagnosed with cancer. While I was sitting by her bedside at MD Anderson, Mom reached over and asked about the ring she had never seen me without. Not wanting to upset her, I told her it was at home because I didn't want to risk breaking down. After Mom passed away, I decided to make some major changes. As God directed, I obeyed. However, one morning I woke up and worried thoughts filled my head. I was greatly burdened and sad. As I walked into the kitchen, I noticed something shiny on our utility room floor. As I came closer, I realized it was the stone I had lost the year before, and it was sitting right on the path where I would walk that morning, which was a completely different location from where I saw it last.

We really did sweep and mop those floors in a year's time! As I reveled in His incredible power, I found myself catching a glimpse of just how much He cares. In light of this world, that stone means very little. In light of my soul, it means even less. But in my heart, that stone is absolutely precious and He knew that. I felt like He was saying, "See what I can do. I've got this. With the most loving kindness imaginable, I've got this."

As Overseer of my soul, I know He's "got me" right in the palm of His hand just as He had Tae when her time here was completed. This means as we strive to be obedient to our Father and follow His path in this life, we can rest knowing that that the Almighty is our Shepherd. As His sheep, we will not be lost in this world no matter how desperate times might seem. Rest assured the Great Shepherd who oversees our souls is a constant in this world of chaos and darkness.

All or None 1 Peter 3:1-2

Wives, in the same way submit yourselves to your own husbands so that, if any of them do not believe the word, they may be won over without words by the behavior of their wives, when they see the purity and reverence of your lives.

We either believe all of it or none of it.

Of my entire Christian journey, submissiveness to my husband has been the most difficult. It was never my intent growing up to marry or have children. My dreams included a life of independence and freedom, not a home and family, but God changed that. He introduced me to someone who made me more than I am, who taught me and challenged me. I knew the first time I saw him I would marry him. Crazy, yes. We married young, 18 and 19, and, against the odds, started building a life together.

After the first seven years, I realized that our perceptions were totally different. He grew up with a single mom who kept an immaculately clean house, and I grew up with my mom and dad married and a dad who could literally fix anything. Neither of us could live up to the other's ideal of marriage. Marriage was wonderful until the other person couldn't live up to our expectations. He wanted a perfectly clean house but didn't want a part in making that happen, and I expected him to be able to fix the car, the washing machine, and the leaky roof. When we began going to church, I started hearing that I was to be submissive. Seriously! Or, my favorite, "subservient."

Thankfully, our God is patient.

I can be very strong-willed; as I studied God's word, I would easily skip over the submission passages. I simply couldn't do the submission thing. But God works on us in layers, in small increments; and I slowly came to realize that this portion of His Word was just as relevant as any of His Word, and I had to trust Him.

I came to realize that God made me strong for a reason, to walk with confidence in the brothels, to look evil in the eye and not flinch, to bury one of my greatest treasures on this earth and be okay.

But He did not make me strong to be strong in my marriage. Instead He gave me a place of refuge here on earth that can be found in my own husband's arms. A place where I can just be and he will protect me.

Satan has created strife within our marriages, especially those in the Church. The footholds we give him are footholds made of pride, and I'm afraid, as women, we are the worst. We either trust God with it all or none at all. I saw as I began to let go and trust, my Travis flourished in ways I had only dreamed, but, even if he hadn't, my part in this was to be obedient to God. Through that, I find freedom. Too many times, I believe we wait for the other person to change first and then we will change. So we continue in a cycle of dysfunction that must make satan proud. But as women of God, we have been told to be different from the world, to be submissive so that they might see.

Let it begin with us. I'm almost ashamed to admit that years ago, I started *The Love Dare* five times and couldn't get through the first week. Then, I thought it was Trav's fault. Now I know it was my own.

Love; above all else, love.

True Beauty 1 Peter 3:3-4

Your beauty should not come from outward adornment, such as elaborate hairstyles and the wearing of gold jewelry or fine clothes. Rather, it should be that of your inner self, the unfading beauty of a gentle and quiet spirit, which is of great worth in God's sight.

We live now in a country where there is never enough. When food is handed out and when supplies are distributed, if you do not fight to the front of the line, you will not get. You will not receive, and, yet, God's Word tells us to have a gentle and quiet spirit.

As women, we are to have a gentle and quiet spirit. This goes against everything that this world will teach us. In order to be loved, you must be skinnier. In order to be respected, you must stand your ground. In order to be happy, you must have the latest fashions. In order to provide the best for your children, they must have the latest trends. In order to be worthy, we must be beautiful. In order to be, we must have, so we continue trying to have it all and trying to get to the next step, only to feel empty and move on to the next big thing. So we sacrifice ourselves again. We sacrifice our families. We sacrifice, all the while telling ourselves that once we get to the next step, we can just be. We justify a life of whirlwind craziness, and the world encourages it. And we continue on, spiraling out of control.

What if we paused? What if we determined to live set apart? We can say "no" to the world and follow Him and Him alone. I remember those people, don't you? I remember seeing kids when I was in school who were different, who lived set apart. And unfortunately, I looked as the world looked and saw what satan wanted me to see. They didn't fit into the world. They chose at all costs to honor the Sabbath. They lived as God has asked us to live and they were ridiculed, ostracized, called crazy. Yet, they were walking as God has called us to walk. I have had to go back and apologize to my fair share of Christians, and the interesting thing was, they didn't care what I thought because they were living only for their worth in God's sight! How shocking it was to me that they did not care what we had all thought. They didn't care that the world didn't embrace them.

87

They knew the One they were serving, and it wasn't me, and it wasn't the world. They did it in the most humble, God-fearing manner. They were not the Christians who were on display, but those who quietly served as He called.

My desires of this world have changed so dramatically, and I pray that God continues, as He promises, the work that He has started in me. I don't want it all. I only want to live worthy of Him, and that means a radical change from who the world would encourage me to be. It means having an inner circle of real believers I can rely on to find Truth even when sometimes there are no words. It means being different and being okay with that, but remaining humble and recognizing that what is being done through me is done by Him. It means not holding tightly to anything but my Father in Heaven and being okay with that.

Be different today. Let's look inside at who we are and find where we follow the world. Let us find where we are not gentle and quiet. I have found some places in my world where I literally cannot be gentle and quiet, not yet anyways, and God has given me the freedom to step aside and wait while He continues to mature me.

So grateful that He is a God of patience and of amazing grace.

Be Wise 1 Peter 3:5-6

For this is the way the holy women of the past who put their hope in God used to adorn themselves. They submitted themselves to their own husbands, like Sarah, who obeyed Abraham and called him her lord. You are her daughters if you do what is right and do not give way to fear.

Wisdom with our words.

As women of God, we are called to be wise and to be submissive to our husbands even with our words. The words we use toward our husbands, as well as the words we use to describe our husbands to our children, our families, our friends and our own hearts.

It is easy to develop martyrdom syndrome, to feel sorry for ourselves and to be submissive outwardly, but use our friends as people who can commiserate with us regarding our lot in life. Maybe he isn't romantic enough, maybe he isn't as handsome as he once was, maybe he doesn't listen or doesn't care, and the list goes on and on.

Or maybe on the outside we pretend that all is perfect, but behind closed doors we meet him with icy stares, cold words and mean hearts. Thinking what? That this will make it even? God calls us to be submissive. Completely.

Acts of obedience. Period. Different from the world. The world will tell us the grass is greener on the other side, yet the same dirt is under the grass on the other side. The deeper we go in any relationship, we will find that everyone, everyone, has flaws.

Early on in our marriage, I hate to say that my first response was to leave. I would get angry, and, instead of talking it out, I would have the desire to walk. Thankfully, God gave me a husband who had lived through a childhood where leaving was the solution, and when he married me, he married for life.

My advice to all couples who are planning to get married is that it is hard work. There will be days when you won't want to love the person beside you, but with God's provision, you will. You will choose to be obedient to the vows you made before God. Satan wants nothing better than to destroy what God has put together. We have the power not to let him. I know, this is not politically correct these days, but we believe it all or not at all.

I am still very much a work in progress. I can't call my Travis "Master" without sounding extremely sarcastic and self-serving, but I try in my actions daily to treat him with reverence, for he, too, is a child of God.

Untainted Love 1 Peter 3:7

Husbands, in the same way be considerate as you live with your wives, and treat them with respect as the weaker partner and as heirs with you of the gracious gift of life, so that nothing will hinder your prayers.

And this is how it is supposed to work. On both sides there is to be reverence for each other. Respect, love, trust, dignity. And this is how in my mind I was able to reconcile the whole submissive text. We have once again taken words that were meant to create good and harmony, a heavenly partnership that results in the greatest team imaginable. By a world tainted by evil, these words have been used to oppress, place women in bondage, beat, damage, subdue and control, sometimes even in the name of God.

No wonder our relationships are where they are. No wonder instead of loving those who have been given to us, we often fear completely trusting them. No wonder our closest relationships may not be with our own mates.

Men. In the same way. In the same way. There is no part in that which suggests she should walk behind you, that she is your property, that you are her master. Sarah called Abraham "Master" out of reverence that was earned, not demanded. She called him "Master" out of obedience to Her Father in Heaven, not because it was demanded from her husband. And, my friends, there is a big difference. It took me a long while to accept the weaker sex thing, but, for the most part, men are physically stronger than women, yes? Physically, they are. There are some men (even my own husband) that I can (and have) gone "toe- to- toe" with. I used to do a few martial arts tournaments, and, at times, would be placed to fight in the men's division. I loved it. Loved the rawness, loved the no drama, no fluff, just game on. I was even placed against my husband and won. Did it mean I was stronger than him? Not at all. Quicker, more agile, more experienced, maybe. But, not stronger. Does it mean as a woman I am less? No.

Again, we have taken words and allowed satan to have a field day manipulating their intent. The greatest partnerships are those that look past the worldly ideas and place their full focus on Christ. Pure focus that results in such a heavenly relationship that the world will take notice and ask how. Men should choose to honor their wives with the purest of hearts, unselfishly loving them in a manner that builds them up to their greatest potential. God will reward. But for those who have bought into the worldly design of using God's words for their own personal pleasure and gain, He tells you here why your prayers aren't being answered.

Love. Simple, pure, untainted love.

Play Nice 1 Peter 3:8

Finally, all of you, by likeminded, be sympathetic, love one another, be compassionate and humble.

He tells us once again to play nice with one another.

We beat each other up so well that it has become almost second nature to us. When someone actually is nice to us, we question their motives. I try to imagine a place where everyone is kind, not just on the outside, but on the inside, too. No stray thoughts, no unkind looks, just loving-kindness. I can't fathom it; it follows that I am unable to comprehend heaven.

I have learned in Nicaragua that a simple smile disarms much. Often times, I have encountered intimidating people, especially men, and a smile typically changes everything. Then they aren't so scary, and neither am I. It doesn't come easy to take the first step, and there may be times that you might be ignored or laughed at, as adults even, yes? But the times when you break down that false barrier between two people to allow precious fellowship, how powerful.

Satan wants us to be everything opposite of what God desires. Be proud. You deserved it. Your kids deserve it. Don't call to check on them. They didn't check on you when you were sick. Don't give him money, for who knows what he might do. Let him sleep on the couch tonight; that's what he deserves. And in the process of trying to protect what is ours, we lose it all.

Will you be taken advantage of? Quite possibly, but maybe it is one step in the journey God has for you. I've had relationships in the past that were drainers of my energy and time. They literally drained and drained me, and they just kept it coming until one day I realized God had developed in me more patience and grace I thought possible.

Let's love.

Forgiveness 1 Peter 3:9

Do not repay evil with evil or insult with insult. On the contrary, repay evil with blessing, because to this you were called so that you may inherit a blessing.

I love that these words were written by Peter. I wonder if he laughed at himself a bit as he wrote this, or did he grimace with remembrance of the times when he quickly repaid evil with evil? Remember when the soldiers came to take Jesus, and Peter quickly drew his sword and cut off the soldier's ear, and, just as quickly, Jesus fixed it. Peter, are you not listening? Have you not seen? Be kind. Don't be evil, too.

One of the best books on forgiveness I have ever read was about an Amish community. When a gunman entered their school and killed some of their own, they appeared that day at the door of the gunman's house giving their forgiveness, refusing to return evil for evil. Choosing to respond differently.

This is large-scale forgiveness, right? But what about the car that cuts us off in traffic? I know people who have different personalities behind the wheel of a car, who demonstrate actions and behaviors they would never do face-to-face. Or what about how we talk to our children and our husbands and wives?

Like Peter, the Holy Spirit has had a lot to work on with me. I've had so many questions. Is evil in response ever justifiable? An insult either thought or spoken ever warranted? The world will say absolutely, but Christ calls us to be different.

Those who are not believers have not been called to live set apart, but as God's children, we have. Expect evil acts toward you. Don't be caught off-guard. Expect to be insulted. Don't be found unaware. Be on guard. Be ready.

Live worthy.

Keeping Peace 1 Peter 3:10-15

For "Whoever would love life and see good days must keep their tongue from evil and their lips from deceitful speech. They must turn from evil and do good; they must seek peace and pursue it. For the eyes of the Lord are on the righteous and his ears are attentive to their prayer, but the face of the Lord is against those who do evil." Who is going to harm you if you are eager to do good? But even if you should suffer for what is right, you are blessed. "Do not fear their threats; do not be frightened. But in your hearts revere Christ as Lord. Always be prepared to give an answer to everyone who asks you to give the reason for the hope that you have. But do this with gentleness and respect.

The majority of our Bible studies are held in areas where we have to be very intentional about logistics. Our games must be selected carefully, the craft and snack prepared and distributed with precision, all in the name of keeping peace. It's a way of life, and it's not a bit passive. In our daily lives, "keeping the peace" has come to mean we've ceased to act or that we are accepting less. Yet, we are told here to seek peace and pursue it. Not just to seek but to pursue. All actions on our part.

It is interesting that the more we delve into God's word, the more we put our desires aside and read His word for what it was truly meant to be, we are reminded once again that the accountability lies directly with our actions. We are to work to create the peace in our world. We don't just pray for it or hope for it. As far as it is concerns us, we each make it happen. It doesn't matter what he did or said. It doesn't matter that they hurt our feelings once again. How can we strive to make peace? Sometimes, it does mean to set our desires aside. It means to look objectively and say, "God's will and not our own."

I walked into the cancer shelter today and my heart fell. I thought I saw Martita sitting in a chair not too far away. Martita was the precious lady who told me about heaven a few days after Taellor had died. Martita died a week after Tae. "Oh, God, no, please, don't let her suffer again here. Not when she's been there," my heart cried out.

And I heard Him say, "And Tae?"

Her, too, Father. Her, too. As much as we miss her. As much as there is an empty place in our hearts, our home, our ministry. Tae, too. On second look, as I slowly drew my eyes to see her again, it wasn't Martita, but another precious grey-haired lady with a big smile and Martita's duster sitting exactly where Martita sat.

Father, keep them where they no longer experience the pain and suffering of this world. Where they will no longer look evil in its face.

With Utter Grace 1 Peter 3:16

Keeping a clear conscious, so that those who speak maliciously against your good behavior in Christ may be ashamed of their slander.

I love that the word 'maliciously' is used here. Not wrongly, not harshly, but maliciously about our behavior. Spoken with the intent of bringing evil and harm.

We are instructed to be gentle, have respect and a clear conscious. Wow. So what about the times when we are wronged intentionally? Gentleness and respect. Again, we are to expect this to happen. We shouldn't be surprised, but be prepared so that we can respond through Christ's love and not our own bare emotions. I can think of two occasions when I have been maliciously attacked by words. I hate to say that both times I was ill-prepared, shocked, and, frankly, quite upset that someone would speak to me with such hate and with such a desire to strip away my dignity.

My response was neither gentle nor respectful; I was indignant. And then today, I come to Peter's writings, and I should have known. It will happen. It will. We fight not against flesh and blood. It goes deeper than that. The Light that shines in you will make those who are not believers feel uncomfortable at times. It just will. Be ready for it. Be gentle, kind and respectful so that when the malicious words make a full circle, they will come up empty, and your accusers will be left with only their false words, and your witness as a believer will still be strong.

One of my situations has come full circle. Until the other one does, I must keep Peter's words hidden in my heart, mind and soul. I think of Christ being ridiculed time and time again. He looked neither right nor left, but stayed focused on the Father so that they, too, might know Him. Even those who cause us the most pain. Even them.

Expect to Suffer 1 Peter 3:17

For it is better, if it is God's will, to suffer for doing good than for doing evil.

From the time we are little kids, we are told that if we treat others nicely, they will treat us nicely in return. If we extend favor, we will receive favor in return, and all is good. Until it is not.

I think we all understand—we may not like it—but we do understand when we dabble in sin, there are consequences, and we suffer. If we lie, if we steal, if we have an affair, if we gossip, if we cheat, if we _____, our trustworthiness and our character suffers. Our witness. We may lose friends, family members or our livelihoods, but we lose due to a choice that we personally make. We lose due to consequences of our actions and this is relatively easy to reconcile in our minds.

But what if we suffer while we are doing good? What if we consciously choose to do good and still we suffer? And what if it is God's will?

From a worldly perspective, it doesn't make sense at all. But I didn't deserve this. But I was trying to help. But I was doing good. And you probably were. Suffering because you were doing good doesn't negate the good motive. Not at all. Our behavior in response to the suffering may, but the suffering itself does not. So again, we are back to us and how we choose to respond.

If we have truly done the act of kindness as service to our Father, a "job well-done" from Him should be plenty, and suffering as a result of that job well-done for the kingdom should encourage us, not hinder us. Satan tries to prevent goodness. He does. How better to throw us off-base than to cause insults to be hurled at us? How better to stop us than to judge our very motives? If we stand ready, armed and clothed in Righteousness, then and only then, will sticks and stones not matter and God will reveal them as the lies they are.

Do goodness today and expect suffering in return.

To Remember 1 Peter 3:18-19

For Christ also suffered once for sins, the righteous for the unrighteous, to bring you to God. He was put to death in the body but made alive in the Spirit. After being made alive, he went and made proclamation to the imprisoned spirits.

We were asked recently by a dear friend what we want to come out of Tae's death. I can tell you what has come out of it. For us, a more intimate understanding of who God is and a better understanding of death: that God gives life and ends life here on this earth. No accidents, no mistakes. A reminder that we are a part of something much bigger than ourselves, and in that part, we can either bring honor to God, or we can advance satan's plans. We have learned that the peace that passes all understanding is surreal and unexplainable. That our decision years ago to try to live more purposefully and with no regrets was part of our preparation for this time. And the list goes on and on. I seriously think I could write "10,000 Reasons" and more on God's faithfulness during this time.

I know that there are many who just don't quite understand how we have continued on. But with God being so evident all around us, how could we not? A small look into one of the many things we have experienced: Sunday at the beach, which was hard at first, I remember praying, "God, just let me find one of her favorite shells." She loved the long, spindled, pointy ones. Not only did we quickly see one, but they just kept appearing! Tae would be excited to find one; rarely did we find two. We see God everywhere. We did before she died and certainly still do.

There are those who say, "It is all in how you look at the situation. You choose to say it is Him that is doing all of this." Okay, no arguments there. We absolutely do choose to see His incredible hand at work, and He is constantly at work. Just like in the days of old, of Abraham, Noah, and Joseph, He still is. We can still have daily, without-ceasing communion with Him. The question is, do we choose to? Do we choose to look beyond the trappings of this world and choose to see Him instead?

99

What we would like others to take away from Tae's death really has nothing to do with her, although as her parents, we think she's pretty incredible and cannot wait to see that incredibleness beyond the confines of a sinful world. But rather we want everyone to remember the quickness, the swiftness, the decisiveness of her passing. We want it remembered that death will come to us all unless we are alive when Christ returns. Each one of us, while we might feel incredibly alive and well, have a time of death already "stamped" on our lives.

Are you okay with yours ending right now? Immediately, our minds go to the physical trappings of this world. Who will take care of my family when I am gone? Who will love on the unloved children and hold them? God will fill in those spaces, but what about your next step? Is it secure? I wake up differently than I did before Tae died. I wake up pondering if today will be my day. It is not from a place of desiring to go on, but rather a desire to live worthy. It comes from a desire to live that on that last day, in that last hour, knowing I will have lived worthy. I know my salvation is secure, but I am still running my race in this world, and each moment is one moment closer to the prize.

Live Worthy 1 Peter 3:20-22

To those who were disobedient long ago when God waited patiently in the days of Noah while the ark was being built. In it only a few people, eight in all, were saved through water, and this water symbolizes baptism that now saves you also--not the removal of dirt from the body but the pledge of a clear conscience toward God. It saves you by the resurrection of Jesus Christ, who has gone into heaven and is at God's right hand--with angels, authorities and powers in submission to Him.

Baptism: demonstrating public obedience to our Father by outwardly demonstrating our belief and faith in Him for all to see.

I remember when Tae was a child and I first realized that she understood and wanted to be a Christian. When young children decide to accept Christ, we hesitate. Do they really believe? Do they really understand? Are they only doing it because they saw someone else do it? I remember questioning her and questioning her. Finally, my precious, strong-willed little girl looked at me and said, "Mom, why can't I believe, too?" Wow. Yes, why can't you believe, too? Let the little children come, and God, help us to overcome the worldliness that tries to make it more complicated than it is. She knew in her heart, she knew.

It was many years later at Camp Barnabus, a special needs camp, when she turned her life over to God, but on that day as a young girl, she became a believer and was baptized. The day that we are baptized there is no question or hesitation about whether or not we are believers. We demonstrated in a fairly outward action our obedience to our Father. Yes, I am a Christian. What if we were to continue that outward demonstration of our faith in our daily lives? Do we mirror Christ in our everyday actions? In the days of Noah, would we be one of the eight that were saved? We talk about how the world today is so evil and times are difficult, but in the days of Noah, only eight found favor. Eight. Can you imagine a world of evil and chaos in which only eight are found worthy?

In Genesis 6, we are told that every inclination of the thoughts of man's heart was only evil all the time. As followers of Christ, we are called to demonstrate our faith in God so that others might know, so that we encourage others to believe, instead of causing them to stumble in their faith quest (Really, he's a Christian?

101

Wow, I didn't realize. She goes to church? That's a surprise.). Everyday actions, everyday thoughts, everyday obedience. Where do we fail in this? Do we fail in this?

In both of our countries, the U.S. and Nicaragua, we can outwardly declare Christ as King as loud and as strong as our heart's desire. We can openly own and read the Bible. We can be baptized in public and not anticipate the burning of our homes or the killing of our families. We have the freedom to study His Word and hide it in our hearts. Why don't we seize the moment? Why don't we? I worry that we are not growing as believers. Our spiritual discipline takes a backseat to life.

But what happens when the day of persecution comes? What happens when the days of openly reading and owning Bibles is no more? Will we be ready? Will our strength be found in God? If we had to recreate the Scriptures on scraps of paper, could we recall it?

I pray that God's protection will fall upon us, but what if this incredible time of religious freedom is actually a time of preparation? Let's not allow material possessions keep us from why we are truly here on this earth. It isn't to buy the biggest house, to always have the newest model of car, to obtain the next promotion. These things are nice and are wonderful blessings, but don't let our blessings become trappings. Start memorizing scripture again. Hide God's Word in our hearts and have it constantly on the forefront of our minds so that when the day comes, Truth is our foundation, no matter what the earthly "foundation" may appear to be.

Live for Him 1 Peter 4:1-2

Therefore, since Christ suffered in his body, arm yourselves also with the same attitude, because whoever suffers in the body is done with sin. As a result, they do not live the rest of their earthly lives for evil human desires, but rather for the will of God.

....but rather for the will of God.

How incredibly different would our lives look if we lived them entirely for the will of God. Entirely. Not just on Sunday morning, not just on religious holidays, not just when we have someone watching, but entirely for the will of God. Nothing else, nothing else matters. Nothing. There may come a time. A day. A moment when the "cost" of following God is more than having to get up early on Sunday or spending half an hour a day reading our Bible. There may come a point in our lives when the cost will be greater. It may be that we will lose our career, our friendships, our way of life, or our very lives, if we choose to continue our journey of faith. I believe when those days come, God will direct our path, our words and our actions, but I also believe that during those times, we will see with clarity what we truly believe. We will see Whose we truly are.

We are told to arm ourselves with the same attitude. If we are done with sin, truly done, satan will take notice of our lives and how we live, and we will suffer. We will. We were not created to live in harmony with this world. However, we tend to avoid pain at any cost. It is easier to avoid than confront, it is easier to stay silent than take a stand, it is easier to walk away than truly bare our souls and love because we might get hurt. But if our sights are on Christ, if we live only focused on Him, evil loses its power over us. It loses its sting and ability to hurt us. When we can live in obedience to Him, we find comfort in doing His work even when it hurts.

A common question we are asked down here is, "How do you do it? How do you see this every day and not just lose it?" Well, there are days when we do just lose it. There are days when what I have seen or experienced truly breaks my heart. There are days when I have to walk away before the tears spill from my eyes, but God is faithful and holds us in the palm of His hand. He lets me walk away, cry for a bit, and then come back, standing ready to love, not in my power, but in His.

103

Is life good today? Is it because we find happiness in being obedient to our Father, or is it because we are fmding solace in the world? If today was your day, if your life ended today, and clarity was revealed, are you good?

Live Different 1 Peter 4:3-4

For you have spent enough time in the past doing what pagans choose to do-living in debauchery, lust, drunkenness, orgies, carousing and detestable idolatry. The are surprised that you do not join them in their reckless, wild living, and they heap abuse on you.

Debauchery: extreme indulgence or decadence for pleasure of the senses.

Lust: a strong sexual desire, or a strong desire for something.

Drunkenness: to be delirious with or as if with strong drink; intoxicated.

Orgies: any actions or proceedings marked by unbridled indulgence of passions.

Carousing: to engage in boisterous, drunken merrymaking.

Idolatry: the worship of an object as a god.

God is telling us again to live differently. Live differently from the world. Live differently from how we lived prior to being Christians. In each of these, the common factor is an extreme way of living that does not have a Godly focus. Extreme indulgence, extreme desire, extreme intoxication, extreme indulgence of passions, extreme merrymaking and worship of something other than the one true God.

I am very much an extremist, if I am not careful. Friends who know me well know this. Whether it be martial arts, yoga, running, reading, working, studying, you name it, I can completely, completely overindulge. Some might call it being an overachiever, but I have come to realize that for me, it is wrong. There is nothing wrong with any of those activities until I let it go to the level past balanced. What is interesting is that I can overindulge in any of these activities and be praised greatly, but when I "overindulge" in my relationship with Christ, I am quickly labeled as radical or cautioned about being too heavenly-minded to be of any earthly good.

105

Through my journey with Christ, I have learned that satan can take a good thing such as a good activity or a good project, and, with my tendencies to overindulge, quickly use it as a way to pull me away from God, pull me from my family, and pull me from my real purposes in life. Just like Eve and the fruit, if I am not careful, I will fall for it every time. Every time. Tae was good about where she focused her time and talents. She schooled me constantly when I would start to veer. I remember after we had moved here to Nicaragua, an opportunity presented itself for her to dance here. It would have required her to be disciplined again in the dance world, spending hours in the studio. I thought of the possibilities of ministry through this talent of hers. Very quickly, she closed that door, knowing full well where God intended her to be and who He called her to minister to. Not looking left or right, but straight ahead toward the journey God had laid before her.

I think many times when we read this verse in 1 Peter, we quickly glance through it and dismiss it. If we drink, we don't drink to excess, or maybe we don't drink at all. We are married with no extramarital affairs, and we don't worship statues, so we are fine. But when we look more closely, we might not dismiss it so easily. If we aren't careful, we live lives of extremes. Where do we spend most of our time? Work? What about our time after work? How much time does God truly get in our lives? If someone else observed our lives for a week, a month, or a year, what would they rank as important in our lives? Where would God rank? Do we truly place Him first? What can we do differently tomorrow that will demonstrate not just to the world, but also to ourselves, that He is the Lord of our life?

Change 1 Peter 4:4

They are surprised that you do not join them in their reckless, wild living, and they heap abuse on you.

Changes. Radical changes.

I used to LOVE Halloween. Loved it. Taellor and Devon have memories of incredible Halloweens. We would all dress up, decorate the house, and host incredible Halloween parties. Once, we created a haunted house and I LOVED it. I had a friend during this time who chose not to participate in Halloween and, oh, the grief that I gave her. "Really? Really? Just think what he is missing? It is just fun! Don't dress him up in scary costumes. Just bring him."

And then, my life changed. I had such an incredible thirst for God's Word and read and read and read. Then I got to Deuteronomy 18:10-12, which says, " Let no one be found among you who...practices divination or sorcery, interprets omens, engages in witchcraft, or casts spells, or who is a medium or spiritist or who consults the dead. Anyone who does these things is detestable to the Lord..." I had to pause. I had an incident with a Ouija Board as a young girl that was pivotal in my thinking, as it was for the dear friend who was with me. I also had an experience that would forever change my view of horror movies and "senseless fun" activities.

Many years after I accepted Christ as my Savior, I answered God's call to go with an evangelistic team to an area of Nicaragua that is steeped greatly in dark magic and voodoo. I found myself again face-to-face with evil. Yet, I had witnessed God's provisions every step of the way, beginning six months prior to the trip. God is faithful. Seeing the evidence of evil in that dark place was truly life-changing. The wide chasm between God's provision and satan's destruction solidified my faith in our Father. I returned from that trip understanding what I already knew to be true. That evil, no matter how pretty, no matter how dressed up or vogue, is evil. It is. And to partake in any of it was wrong.

And, oh, the grief that I caught from our kids (We've always done it before! Why not now?") to our friends ("What's the big deal? Do Trunk and Treat. It is church sponsored."). And I caved until I met a real witch. Yes, a real witch. Do you tell your children that they are a fantasy? They are very much alive and well. And then I knew in my heart of hearts that I had to answer for my own obedience: "As for me and my household, we will serve the Lord" (Joshua 24:15). Now I live in a country where they think it is absolutely crazy that we would celebrate Halloween. It seems absolutely crazy to them that we would dress up as devils, witches and ghosts, much less dress up and parade our most precious treasures as them.

When we make changes, what the world considers "radical" changes, we will be messed with. We will. Be ready. And the opposition can be fierce. Your changes may force them to reevaluate their lives, and that isn't always welcomed. Be obedient, but be obedient humbly. Walk with assurance, yet walk softly. Life isn't a popularity contest. Odds are there may be more who dislike you than truly like you, and, as the end draws near, this will become even more apparent. So stand ready, armed with God's word, obedient in every step. (By the way, I have since apologized profusely to my sweet friend over the Halloween incident!)

The Race of Our Lives 1 Peter 4:5

But they will have to give account to him who is ready to judge the living and the dead.

There will come a day when there are no more tears, no more pain, and no more fears; and there will be a day of judgment, even for believers. Our salvation is secure; rest assured in that, but our activities here on this earth will be judged. How have we lived? Have we lived worthy? Have our days, moments and talents been used for the Kingdom? Will we hear, "Well done, good and faithful servant," or will we squeak by, resting only on our salvation?

I remember my worldview before I became a Christian. The judgment day my world focused on was the judgment between heaven and hell. As I further delved into God's word, I came to realize that there would be another judgment for believers, one for our work done in this world, and this frightened me to my core. I have been given so much: freedom of religion, freedom of education, abundance of food and other material securities that the majority of the world does not enjoy. I have the freedom of speech and as many Bibles as I could ever want. Do I use them to the fullest potential that I can? I do not.

God has given us such an incredible opportunity. I have heard many people complain about the difficulties of being a Christian today in the U.S., but, truthfully, I see such opportunities for us as Christians born in America. We have such freedom and such capability. May we use our freedom and gifts to further His kingdom, not to seek our own agenda. The day is coming; for some of us, it may come sooner than others. Each day, each moment, brings that time closer. We will stand before the Father to be judged according to the many blessings and freedoms that we have been given, and the way we invested them.

Be ready. Run the race of your life. Don't settle for just being invited to the race. Run to win the prize.

Do it Anyway 1 Peter 4:6

For this is the reason the gospel was preached even to those who are now dead, so that they might be judged according to human standards in regard to the body, but live according to God in regard to the spirit.

There are so many questions, right? What about those who died before Christ? What about those who never hear? What about _____? This verse tells us that even those who died before Christ were given the opportunity to know. Even them. God's word is true. If we believe, we believe all or not at all. Yes?

I had an interesting night last night. I listened to someone who shares many of my ideals, like, "Take me to the one who suffers the most," and "Take me to the downtrodden." Where we differ is the purpose and reason behind what we do. I do it so that others might know Him and, through that, will find eternal life and purpose for the world today. I believe that love should be our response to our world, love that comes through me from Him. He uses me, but it isn't about me. It isn't. No matter which way the wind might blow, no matter how things end or begin, it is not about me. More of Him and less of me to the point where I am a mere shadow shining amidst a great Light. A shadow that will always be judged by men while I am on this earth.

I find I face about ten times more criticism as a missionary than I did as a sonographer or educator. We are told to expect that, and I am here to testify that it is true. How we share love doesn't always fit the mold. I walk confidently, knowing that my judge is not that person who hurls criticism my way. My judge is my heavenly Father, and He is a good judge.

Walk today in boldness. Walk today knowing that as you love in Christ's name, you will be criticized. Do it anyway.

In the Journey 1 Peter 4:7

The end of all things is near. Therefore be alert and of sober mind so that you may pray.

I have to be completely honest: ever since Taellor's departure from this earth (her death, her passing, whatever label we want to put on it), I have had to resist hanging a sign around my neck that reads, "The end is near." I know there is a fine line between being passionate and being labeled so crazy that no one will listen. But, listen, listen, not just with your ears, but your very soul. The end is near. Whether our end comes with the return of Christ or through physical death, it is near. Be prepared, be ready, always.

What controls your mind today? What do you think about? God? The kingdom? How much time today will you spend in your Bible reading His words? The end is near, dear friend. It simply is.

I have been asked by several people, "How do I experience God? I feel Him on the mission field, but not in my own life. He isn't doing anything."

Abraham waited a long time for his promised son. A very long time. God was working all those years, preparing him to be the father of that son and preparing his character. We tend to look at our lives and note only the places where we see action, but character is built on the journey, in the quiet disciplines and in the moments when satan whispers to us that our God is not even there.

How do we respond? Do we give into the doubts, or do we push them aside and forge on, knowing that God is working? He is always working, but we have to do our part. We have to say, "No matter what, I will choose to follow Him. I will be obedient, no matter what, always, even in the quiet."

It's coming. Be ready.

Real Hearts 1 Peter 4:8

Above all, love each other deeply, because love covers over a multitude of sins.

Love, love, love.

When we show love, a multitude of our sins are covered. Our sins. Not our neighbor's, not our family's, not our enemy's, but our own sins against others are covered.

It begins with us. We can only control ourselves. We can choose to respond out of love, or out of selfishness. Our choice.

But what if it doesn't come naturally to love certain people, those who hurt us, talk bad about us to others, call us names, or physically abuse us; how do we love them? And what would that love even look like?

I recently read Corrie Ten Boom's book, *The Hiding Place,* which describes how Corrie's sister allows Christ's love to flow through her even amidst the greatest of adversity. What a testimony. I look at Christ and the cross: from His trial to the end, only love.

It is other-worldly. It is God. It is choosing to say, "I forgive," or continuing to pray for those who have hurt you. Love is so much more than valentines and romance. We are told in 1 Corinthians 13 that "[L]ove is patient, love is kind. It does not envy, it does not boast, it is not proud. It does not dishonor others, it is not self-seeking, it is not easily angered, it keeps no record of wrongs. Love does not delight in evil but rejoices with the truth. It always protects, always trusts, always hopes, always perseveres. Love never fails."

We often hear this read at weddings, and I'm afraid because of this, we set it aside for love between husbands and wives. But nothing says that this section is reserved for marriages only. This is love. This is how we are called to respond in every act, every gesture in our life. And what I LOVE is that a lot of love is refraining from doing something bad!

So, when I am wronged, I show love when I don't respond in anger. I don't have to become best friends with this person, I don't have to hug and make up when I don't even want to touch the other person. No, love, true love, is allowing Christ to work through us, not showing worldly love but Godly love. And there is a difference.

Let's watch our actions today. Love.

True Hospitality 1 Peter 4:9

Offer hospitality to one another without grumbling.

I'm too busy. Our house isn't big enough. We've had a long week. The kids are cranky. We haven't gone to the grocery store this week. I haven't had a shower yet. The game's on TV. There is always a good reason not to offer hospitality to our friends and neighbors. Yet, real hospitality, the hospitality that Peter talks about, isn't entertaining guests in our homes; it is more than that. It is inviting them in when they come to our door and offering them what we have to offer. It is inviting them over when the Holy Spirit prompts us even when we have a million personal reasons not to do so. We focus on them. We focus on their needs and not our own.

Of course, this is what we do when we entertain people at our houses, yes? We bring out our best food and dishes. We bring out our very best for them to experience. But what about when you haven't planned, when it isn't your idea, when your best isn't ready to be presented or can't even be found? House is messy? Kids unruly? Only water to drink? What about then? This is when I believe true hospitality comes alive. For some of us, it comes easy. For the rest of us, we must allow Christ to work through us in order to allow it to happen.

I've seen vast differences in hospitality while living here. For those who have come to serve with us down here, you've experienced it. The hospitality extended even though material possessions are minimal. The warmth extended even though furniture is sparse. The sharing of food even when it isn't plentiful. Is this how we do hospitality? All the time? Yes, some of it is cultural, but that is only the type of offering-tortillas as opposed to pie.

We are all called to help meet the needs of those God sends our way, and we are called to do it without grumbling. A place to stay (even if just for a moment), something to eat or drink (even if it is all we have) or just a listening ear. We are called to be Christians, salt and light in a dark world, His hands and feet, 24 hours a day, 7 days a week. It is not a 9 to 5 gig. It doesn't end with the evening news.

Hebrews 13:2 reminds us that we shouldn't forget to "show hospitality to strangers, for by so doing some people have show hospitality to angels without knowing it." And that's pretty cool. Remember, it really isn't about us at all. Never has been.

Gifted By the Father 1 Peter 4:10

Each of you should use whatever gift you have received to serve others, as faithful stewards of God's grace in its various forms.

This is where we waste a lot of time. What gift has God bestowed on us? What category does it fit in? What is the best quiz to take to identify it, to reconfirm it or to identify another one because we don't like the initial results.

We analyze and analyze and analyze; all the while, the very gifts that He has given us wait, and the world moves on in spite of our inaction.

We know when we are around someone gifted by the Father in preaching or teaching. Watching them do what God has created them to do is to experience a bit of heaven on earth. Tae's gift was with children, and not just any children, but children with special needs. I've seen her walk into a room so full of need it would reduce most men and women to tears, and that is where she would shine the brightest. I don't ever remember her taking a quiz to figure it out, but I remember one time after our Special Friends Class at Ridgecrest Baptist Church, she said with the biggest smile, "That is what heaven will be like!" That is where she felt closest to God. Always did.

God gave us gifts and talents to go and do, to use them to serve others, to further His kingdom and His Name. I'm not saying that it is wrong to seek guidance and help if you are having difficulty finding where you fit, but I do think most of us have a pretty clear idea where that is. It is that place where you feel like this is what you were created to do. Truthfully, it is probably not the most glamorous, popular or recognizable deed, but it is the deed that is recognized by the King. I find that it is in moments apart from others, in quiet corners, cardboard houses or among mounds of trash, day in and day out, that I see God's hand upon my life. Perseverance when no one is looking, when the days run together, and the faces become more and more familiar. Does the desire to reach beyond normal boundaries count as a spiritual gift? I don't know, but I do know that God blessed me with this desire from a young age, and this is where I feel closest to Him. This is where I feel in my spirit, "This is what I was created to do."

So what is it? What talent do you have that God has given you to further His kingdom? If you already know it, are you using it to its potential? Do you hide it while waiting for the perfect opportunity to use it? Do you help your children identify their talents and help them explore ways they can use them for God's glory?

Is it Mine to Fight? 1 Peter 4:11

If anyone speaks, they should do so as one who speaks the very words of God. If anyone serves, they should do so with the strength God provides, so that in all things God may be praised through Jesus Christ. To Him be the glory and the power for ever and ever. Amen.

I am stuck in bed with a fever, headache, respiratory something and an unidentified rash on my belly. I am writing this on Tuesday, my favorite day of the week. The day I can serve with wild abandonment. The day we go to House of Hope for Tuesday morning outreach and share God's love with girls and children caught up in the evil of sex trafficking. Lunchtime is spent at the feeding center at the dump, sharing food and God's Word. The afternoon ends with sharing Christ's love with the ladies at the Cancer Shelter, ladies who are oftentimes at death's very door. Today, I am here in bed surrounded by tissues. Tissues that are cleaning up sneezes but also tears. Tears are flowing for a multitude of reasons: a world of sin; a daughter no longer here; children abused, starving, neglected and sexually-assaulted; and the list goes on and on. I find myself stalled, today anyway. Held in one place, alone. This did not occur without a fight, I might add. I was dressed, ready to go, tubs packed and loaded in the truck. I had even dropped Slate off at school, all the while knowing I could not fight through the day. But was I supposed to?

Was it my day to fight? Was I pushing on in my own strength or God's? As I read and reread this verse, allowing God's word to surround me, I realized that while God has given me wonderful gifts, today, He has not given me the strength. Not today. As I made my way back to the house and climbed into bed, I knew I was where I was supposed to be today. I knew it before I went to bed last night, yet, in my humanity, I knew that I could trudge on, that I could complete the day. But the strength I would have been using was my own, not God's, and in the world we live in, the world we serve in, I do not want to walk this journey in my own strength.

There is nothing that needed to be accomplished today that God could not nor would not accomplish without me. Nothing. On most days, He allows me to walk the journey of His work, He allows me to take part,

He allows me to be the recipient of many hugs and loves that are truly His, not mine. Too many times, we trudge on. We trudge on from a place of guilt, responsibility, debt, pride or control. Yet, God tells us that what we do, how we serve, how we use the gifts He has given us, should be accomplished in His strength, not ours. Not ours.

Being still is a hard one for me. I do much better now than I did in the past. I used to push this earthly body way past its limits, all in the name of a deadline. But I have experienced the strength that comes from the Father, and the human pales in comparison. Pales.

That's where I want to be. That's how I want to serve in God's will, using that strength that He provides to accomplish work for His Kingdom. Nowhere in that phrase is the word "me." We serve as He directs, with His strength, not our own.

Where in our lives are we hitting brick walls? Are we hitting them because they are walls we ourselves are fighting? Are we working in our own strength or God's? Do we really think that our world would cease to move if we took a day off just to be? I can tell you that it doesn't. It won't. Even the day when my world came to a screeching stop, the moment when Tae died, the world kept moving. If you feel like you are going crazy trying to survive, if you have to numb yourself to make it through the day, if you don't feel the joy that surpasses all understanding, stop. Choose to make a change in your life that will stop the craziness.

Today, I was reminded yet again that this is not my fight but His. His glory, His strength. His.

Thankful to be a small part of His work.

Do Not be Surprised 1 Peter 4:12

Dear friends, do not be surprised at the fiery ordeal that has come on you to test you, as though something strange were happening to you.

Do not be surprised and, yet, we always are when pain comes our way.

We seek and seek to make heaven on earth, to make happiness here, and then we feel betrayed when evil slips through the cracks of our happy facade. This world, this earth, is not our home. This is not it. We are told in Matthew 10:16, "I am sending you out like sheep among wolves. Therefore be as shrewd as snakes and as innocent as doves." Imagine sending sheep out into a pack of wolves. That is how we have been sent. We have a Shepherd who is protecting us and watching over us, but this will be messy and painful, so we shouldn't be surprised when struggle comes our way.

I vividly remember the first time that I experienced being "among wolves." Many years ago, I was part of a church where I witnessed incredible wrongdoing. Wrong from a secular, business standpoint and, undoubtedly, wrong from a Biblical viewpoint. As I sat literally in disbelief, I was assured that this is quite common and this is simply how it is done. In my world of corporate America, this would not fly and yet, under the guise of "the Church," it was common practice. As a relatively new believer experiencing how the body of Christ worked, I can tell you this was not what I expected to find. Yet, I am thankful that God allowed me to experience that when I did. I didn't understand it at the time, but He was teaching me early on that being sheep among wolves is everywhere, and, just because you find yourself among wolves, you don't ever stop being sheep. Ever.

For while you are treading among the wolves, there are other sheep traveling your same path needing encouragement, fellowship and reaffirmation that God is in control, even in this. Too often, we experience bad things within the Church. We get hurt. Expect it. In heaven, we will serve in a place where there is no evil. We won't get hurt there. Here, we will. And I believe satan revels in this.

There is no better way to distract a Kingdom builder than to create issues within the Church itself. Hurt feelings can fester for years and years, and, instead of placing our energy on Kingdom building, we focus on getting even with our sister or brother in Christ, or at least waiting until they make the first move to apologize.

Or better yet, we stop going all together. We walk away from it all. And truthfully, the way I have seen some treated by "church people," I get it. But when we walk away, when we say the persecution is too much, satan wins every time. I think of our fellow brothers and sisters in Christ who face persecution in the form of death and then think, "Really, we let ourselves be run off from our Father's house because of gossip and haughty looks?" Shame on us. May God strengthen our desire to know Him more so that nothing could keep us away. Nothing. Be the peacemaker. Be the sheep. Follow where the Good Shepherd tells you to go. Expect pain in this world no matter where you are; then, when the blessings of happiness come instead, they are blessings overflowing.

A Privilege 1 Peter 4:13

But rejoice inasmuch as you participate in the sufferings of Christ, so that you may be overjoyed when his glory is revealed.

I am humbled by this verse and not the least bit qualified to speak on its behalf. Christ has blessed us beyond measure. Beyond measure. In 2002, when we decided to come to this country called Nicaragua, we had no idea how our lives would be impacted and changed in an instant. God gave us a glimpse of the future land that He would call us to. From 2002-2007, He allowed us the privilege to return again and again, each time reaffirming the call, each time leaving a part of what seemed like my very soul when I flew home. Then in 2007, it stopped. We spent the years from 2007-2011 being prepared. We didn't know at the time those trials were changing us. We didn't know at the time that He was preparing us to live here. It might have been so much easier (in human hindsight, yes?) to have walked through Travis almost dying, Slaton being born 3 months premature, and my mother being diagnosed and dying of cancer, if we had known that Nicaragua was the plan, and that in 2012, we were going to be given the opportunity to move here and serve Him here. But He had a plan, and He saw the big picture the whole time.

Our serving here is not a sacrifice at all, rather, it's the greatest privilege we have ever known. We don't have the big picture. We have what we can see today, this instant, and even that isn't always a clear picture, but a picture seen through our own perspective. We have no idea what the future will hold. We have conjecture, hopes and dreams, but the reality is He knows and we do not. If you are not a believer, it will be difficult to fathom God's omniscience. Grasping it will give you the ability to say, "I live for today and today alone. God prepares tomorrow, not I."

Our son, Slaton, has Asperger's, and one of the traits he displays is believing that you are thinking as he is; so if he thinks something, it is so. Not exactly. Just because he had a thought that he wanted a glass of chocolate milk, it doesn't mean that I should be handing him one. We work on this, trying to make him aware that the reality is not what he simply thinks. And the same is true, I'm afraid, for us.

122

The reality of our world is not what we simply think it should be. It is what it is. Period. Sure, we can plan, day-dream, plot and make elaborate schemes, but the reality is that we must hold all of this loosely, knowing that our blueprints are our human desires, not true reality. And we mustn't be let down when they don't come to fruition.

When we suffer for Him, we suffer knowing that He will be revealed. Our brothers and sisters in Christ who lay down their very lives for Him know the ultimate earthly price, and yet, this is where we find the body of Christ growing, not waning. This is where we find Truth being held as the most treasured prize, not in lukewarm gratitude, or, dare I say, entitlement.

Stand Worthy 1 Peter 4:14

If you are insulted because of the name of Christ, you are blessed, for the Spirit of glory and of God rests on you.

May we stand worthy. It seems that we spend more of our time being politically correct with our beliefs so that insults don't come our way. I believe it is time to stop and really take a look at the way we live our lives and influence others.

Stand firm, stand ready.

Glory First, Always 1 Peter 5:1-4

To the elders among you, I appeal as a fellow elder and a witness of Christ's suffering who also will share in the glory to be revealed: Be shepherds of God's flock that is under your care, watching over them--not because you must, but because you are willing, as God wants you to be; not pursuing dishonest gain, but eager to serve; not lording it over those entrusted to you, but being examples to the flock. And when the Chief Shepherd appears, you will receive the crown of glory that will never fade away.

Example. Our everyday lives are examples to the flock, and our actions speak volumes.

But what if we are having a bad day? What if someone just cut us off in traffic? What if someone just upset our child? Stepped on our toes? Crossed the line? What then?

I believe that when it is truly the hardest, and when we have to fight literally against our very flesh, that is when the flock notices. Notices that we are different, notices that while we do sin, we do not sin without a heart that is convicted. Through this, they come face-to-face with God.

Our motives must be pure at all times. Even when our back is against the wall or we are left in a place of trust, we must live in a way that brings glory to Him. We don't see the big picture or why we are being positioned where we are. We learn that if we let Him, He will lead.

So take notice of the flock around you; they are positioned among wolves. Guide them for His honor; love them for His glory. They are all His.

Live worthy.

Boxes 1 Peter 5:5

In the same way, you who are younger, submit yourselves to your elders. All of you, clothe yourselves with humility toward one another, because, "God opposes the proud but shows favor to the humble."

I've never liked boxes. I am, actually, quite a rule follower (hard to believe for those who know me well), but boxes people try to put me in, I've never fit. Never.

I've tried and failed miserably. Frankly, before I turned my life over to Christ, I saw Christianity as the biggest box ever. This is how you sit. This is how you talk. This is what you wear. Rules and regulations that I so did not want to follow. I tried, I tried, I tried, and I failed. Don't hear me wrong, this is not how it is everywhere or with all Christians, but I think satan takes this box and highlights it for those who are seeking and even as a Christian seeking, to distract them from the truth. And for Christians seeking to find acceptance in church and its people instead of God, he uses the box to detour us from real faith.

Some of us run from the box, refusing to be put in a box, while others find safety in the box. Either way, it pulls us away from God.

And then I saw God for who He truly is. Christ came and gave us an example to follow, and He didn't fit in a box. He showed us how to live according to the Father. Humbly. Not prideful, not entitled, but humbly. He showed me it was okay to choose to live in a world so much different than my own, to reach into the darkness, following His light and the beat of my own drum.

Today, for those feeling squished into a box, look full into God's face. You will find love and grace there. Your Creator sees you as one of His greatest creations.

Seek Knowledge.....Carefully 1 Peter 5:6

Humble yourselves, therefore, under God's mighty hand, that he may lift you up in due time.

After Tae died, I started reading through the books she had enjoyed reading. I started with the *Giver Trilogy* and proceeded to the *Divergent Trilogy*. In the *Divergent Trilogy*, we are introduced to a world divided into fractions. Four in fact, each with its own distinguishing characteristics. Every one fits perfectly into one of the four except for the divergents, who have good qualities of combinations of the fractions.

One of the groups holds knowledge as the most important of all. Not just knowledge itself, but the quest for knowledge overrides everything else. Experiences are collected like notches on a belt, and if the experience ends up helping someone else, that's an added notch, and not for the one being helped. Self-worth becomes defined by all that I know about anything and everything.

Are we not the same if we aren't careful? If we don't humble ourselves before Him? Are we building our own tower of Babel? Are our "Bucket Lists" for us or for Him? For us or for the Kingdom? For us or for those still seeking?

We will be lifted up out of our humble position. God tells us in His Word that this will happen. Our reward will come in due time, but I have a feeling His reward is more satisfying than any earthly reward we could possibly fathom.

Seek knowledge humbly. Seek experiences humbly.

Seek Him above all else always.

Cast Your Cares 1 Peter 5:7

Cast all your anxiety on him because He cares for you.

How much time and energy do we spend on anxiety? On worry? On sleepless nights? On worldly drama?

Simply, "because He cares." He cares so I can give it all to Him. Praise His Name.

No longer do I have to lay awake at night going over a multitude of possible scenarios.

No longer do I worry about it all.

I lay it at His feet and I walk in His obedience. I choose to serve Him instead, to walk faithfully day by day.

I don't have to control it all, only do the part He has given me and only me to do.

And in that I find peace, finally.

Because He cares.

Even in the days and nights when it seems the very hounds of hell are at my door.

He cares.

128

Prey 1 Peter 5:8

Be alert and of sober mind. Your enemy the devil prowls around like a roaring lion looking for someone to devour.

When I was younger, I read this verse and thought of "the great and mighty lion" prowling for its prey, but as I have gotten older, I've learned more about the lion's hunting patterns. Lions typically will forgo the strongest animal when there is a surer kill such as a weak or injured prey. They search with calculated moves to seek out those that have been separated from the pack, taking them away from the only protection they might have had.

From personal experience, I know satan acts this way in our lives. When I am down, sick, lonely or desperate, I am most vulnerable to his attacks and his lies. When I am strong, I have the energy and confidence to tell him to step aside, but when I am weak, my resistance is low. I will never forget one particularly frightening time when we were at the lake fishing. Trav and I were arguing about something and I let my emotions get the best of me. I decided that I'd show him and go off on my own. I found a placc in the cliffs where I could sit on a towel and my feet would touch the bottom of a ravine (a chair of sorts, yes, a short chair!). As I stood in the ravine positioning the blanket, with my mind reliving the fight with Travis, I heard the warning rattle of a snake. Looking down quickly, I saw a large rattlesnake by my feet. The snake wasn't there when I had first checked the area. He must have moved in while I was distracted. His intent at that moment was to hurt me, and, being that we were in Pontiac, Missouri, deep in the lake area, I was in trouble. I jumped out of the ravine screaming for Travis and running to him for safety (like the snake was really chasing me). That afternoon, I realized the parallel: the isolation, the assumption that all is well, the distraction, the deadliness that was waiting.

I know when we are hurting the worst; we tend to want to isolate ourselves, because of embarrassment, sadness, hurt feelings and pride. And in our weakness, satan begins his attack in earnest. Picking at us, hurting us when we are the most defenseless. And, dear ones, we need to remember that he doesn't come to us as a lion or a serpent, but as the most subtle, effective deceiver. Be careful.

IX!hen you are most weak, when you are struggling and the darkness is closing in, run to God. Run to those who are Christ-like. Find shelter in the Lord Most High.

Bucket List 1 Peter 5:9

Resist him, standing firm in the faith, because you know that the family of believers throughout the world is undergoing the same kind of sufferings.

In light of persecution in the news today, this humbles me greatly. Our brothers and sisters in Christ are facing persecution ranging from isolation to death. Families are standing strong in their faith. They are standing on a faith that was built on a strong foundation. They are standing on the faith that can only come through a true relationship with God.

We are building our foundations today. In a time of rest, we are to be building the kind of faith that will stand when persecution comes our way. True faith. We ask, "What can we do?" when we hear the news of persecution around the world. Here Peter tells us: Resist the devil and stand strong. What does that look like in our world? Stand strong. Make a daily commitment to pray and read our Bibles. Fellowship with other believers. Encourage one another in our faith. Be Christ's hands and feet and show love to a world that is starting not to recognize the purity of love. Resist the devil. Don't give in to his temptations. The first step is the hardest. Begin today. Beware, he comes. Yet, we serve the One who has overcome it all.

At some point in time, it will be too late to make our faith a priority. Time is not on our side, so our urgency to cross items off our spiritual bucket list should be as real as that of our physical one.

Stand firm. Stand strong. Stand real.

Seek Him…..Full-On 1 Peter 5:10

And the God of all grace, who called you to His eternal glory in Christ, after you have suffered a little while, will Himself restore you and make you strong, firm and steadfast.

Let's read that again: "And the God of all grace, who called you to His eternal glory in Christ, after you have suffered a little while, will Himself restore you and make you strong, firm and steadfast."

And that is a promise that comforts me, that gives me the strength to continue on, to look past the reality and solidly hold onto His promise. Amidst the hunger, trash, dirt, disparity, broken promises from this world, and hurtful words and glances, God tells us that this will only last a little while and He, Himself, will restore us.

Some of us by death, some by His Second Coming.

Hold on. It's coming. It seems as if the darkness will last an eternity. Satan's lies will tell us it will, but the only thing that will last an eternity is eternal life found through Christ.

I know so many are suffering now. I'm sorry for your pain. I am. I'm sorry we are in a world that revels in brokenness, but we are where we are, and, in this brokenness, the only Light that can break through the despair is Christ's.

Seek Him full-on.

132

Not Brainwashed...Really it is God 1 Peter 5:11

To Him be the power for ever and ever. Amen.

This is all about Him. The Kingdom. There was a time in my life when it was all about me, my family, my desires, my wants and me, me, me, me. During that time, I found (and this is where I should say despair and unhappiness) happiness. Life was good. We took the next step in life, and the next and the next. God had no part in our thoughts.

And then we began to understand more about Christ and who He really is. This world, this universe became much bigger than I ever imagined, and life took on a completely different meaning. It was no longer about me, us or we, but Him.

Some who read this will scream CRAZY. Some will go so far as to say we are brainwashed. I was there once, too, and thought those same thoughts. I also know that no amount of defense or arguing from any man was going to change my mind.

I watched the lives of those who were real believers, and I found God where they were serving.

And once I experienced Him for who He is, I knew.

And I could easily say, "All power to Him forever."

Even in the midst of human tragedy.

All Power to Him forever.

Kiss of Love 1 Peter 5:12-14

With the help of Silas, whom I regard as a faithful brother, I have written to you briefly, encouraging you and testifying that this is the true grace of God. Stand fast in it. She who is in Babylon, chosen together with you, sends you her greetings, and so does my son Mark. Greet one another with a kiss of love. Peace to all of you who are in Christ.

Greet one another with a kiss of love.

The greeting is one of my favorite customs of Nicaragua. It's not just a handshake or a hug or a formal kiss; it's a kiss of love. I have become so accustomed to this practice that when I visit the States, I have to hold myself back from kissing those I love.

This is the conclusion of 1 Peter. Tomorrow, we move on to 2 Peter as we continue to work through the verses that Tae left Annie over a year ago. There are so many hurting out there with broken hearts and lost dreams. I encourage you, yet again, to turn to face Him fully. Do not look left or right, do not allow the world to have any room in your thoughts. Lean on the true grace of God. There is more than just this. We were created to overcome death. We are children of God, and yet we let ourselves become burdened by the ways of this world. We spend time focusing on and fretting about matters that have no lasting bearing on eternity or even tomorrow.

Build relationships with people, because that is what lasts. Does it really matter who wins or loses an argument? In the midst of the battle, in the midst of the pouting, in the midst of avoiding each other, satan revels in the absence of fellowship between God's creations. He attempts to isolate us and then fills our mind with lies, and they are lies. Friends, if something comes into your mind that is not godly, figure out the source of the thought. 1 Peter has challenged us about how we should live, and 2 Peter will continue; yet, the real question is: What is our response? When the trumpet sounds, it will be instantaneous. It won't be like New Year's Eve that makes its way around the world.

Let's live ready.

134

2 Peter

In 1 Peter, Peter wrote to encourage us. He wrote to encourage those undergoing persecution, suffering and hardship. He wrote to encourage those in the midst of the storm. In 2 Peter, he is writing to warn us of complacency and heresy. There are some things that are simply nonnegotiable. It is what it is. There are false teachers who will try to negotiate faith, who will try to water it down, to change and twist it, but the Word of God stands as it is. Always. When Tae left these verses with Annie, I wonder what was going through her mind. I have come to believe that she might not even have realized why she was writing these down but was merely being obedient. Listening and following, even when it doesn't make sense. They were not on her list of "go-to" verses. They were not verses that she had memorized and held dear to her heart. These were verses that He gave to her for such a time as this. For us now.

Persecution, suffering and hardship come from the world. Complacency and heresy, we can control. We allow ourselves to become complacent, to walk daily without really living as we were called to live. We listen to false teachers when we could walk away. When they are saying what we wish to hear. We have the power to walk away. We have the power to refuse to become complacent, to refuse not to be used to our full potential.

I look at my own life, and I see areas where I am complacent. Physically, I am not where I should be. If my body is my temple, I am doing a horrible job of taking care of the temple. Complacent. Time with the Father. I consistently have quiet time with the Father, but lately I have been challenged about how I use it. I typically do a Bible Study, which is me completing a task. What about me just being with Him? Just being. Frankly, it intimidated me at first, just to be. No reading, no writing, no verse to memorize or song to sing; just the Father and me with no other distractions.

Tomorrow, we delve into 2 Peter; today, let's examine the question, "Where are we complacent in life?" Why? It is time to move, to change, to love.

Direct Measure 2 Peter 1:1-2

Simon Peter, a servant and apostle of Jesus Christ, To those who through the righteousness of our God and Savior Jesus Christ have received a faith as precious as ours: Grace and peace be yours in abundance through the knowledge of God and of Jesus our Lord.

Grace and peace be ours. In abundance. That's what we want, isn't it? Lots of grace in our world so that when we mess up or we step out of line, we are covered in grace. Grace from our Father, our family, our friends, our teachers. A life covered in grace followed by lots of peace. Pure peace. Peace throughout our lives, our family, our city, our churches, our community, our land, our nation and our world. Peace. But how do we get that?

"Grace and peace be yours in abundance through the KNOWLEDGE of God and of Jesus our Lord." Based on this, based on how much knowledge we have of God and of Jesus our Lord, how much grace should be in our lives? Based on how much knowledge we have of God and of Jesus our Lord, how much peace should be in our lives? Or maybe we work backwards: How much grace is in our life? An abundance? Mediocre? A little? And this reflects the knowledge that we have of Him. What about peace? How much peace is in our world? An abundance? Overflowing? None? Again, a reflection of the knowledge that we have of Him.

As we walk through 2 Peter, he reminds us not to take any of this lightly. I find it quite pertinent that I am in 2 Peter right now. When Tae left the verses to us, the initial verses helped us deal with the initial shock, the initial, "Wow, I know I believe, but Wow." 1 Peter helped us deal with the struggle of her absence, the struggle of a life with a different focus, a life with a different sound and a different look. Now, at a time when we see this life as it is, and we walk in obedience, God is reminding us through Peter not to become complacent. Don't forget the pain of losing Tae, but balance it with the awesomeness of Who He is. Don't remember her death and the emptiness of her room and forget Whose she is. Read our Bibles more, sit and just be with Him and listen to His voice. If you aren't hearing Him, figure out why not. Look and see where He is working and go there. Go be a part of His work.

136

Shiny Things 2 Peter 1:3

His divine power has given us everything we need for a godly life through our knowledge of him who called us by His own glory and goodness.

It can seem a mystery. It can seem out of this world, crazy, unbelievable, until we start to seek Him in knowledge through praying, reading His word and spending time just being. When was the last time that happened? Just being in His presence.

This week, we've been in the US and it has been such a blessing. God has blessed me with friends who are like family, and we come together and share in life. We share in our loss of Tae in this world; and their loss of husbands, fathers and mothers. We share in the passion to do what we can to make a difference while we are here, not for a title or recognition, but because it is right. I love that. God has blessed me with some incredible mentors and mentees. We don't have to do this on our own. We can try and we might succeed; some of us are just "dogged" enough to do so, but there's no good reason to go it alone.

As I shared with a group last night, one of the things I will forever remember about the loss of Tae from this world was how sudden and final it was. There was no turning back; there was no time for recognition of "What now?" or "What is out there on the other side?" It just was. So if you have the slightest thought of what if? Or is it really? Or even, could it really be? Seek answers. I had to seek before I could believe, and, once I started seeking, I knew that I had found Truth. Truth that would ground me during some of the most tragic craziness of this world. Truth that allows me to serve in some of the most desolate areas of the world and see the potential for hope found only through Christ.

For those of us who are already believers, is our knowledge of Him overflowing into our world? Do people see Him through you? Not judgment but love. That's why we were called. Be cautious in a world that will cover Truth with all things shiny.

137

No Days Off 2 Peter 1:4

Through these he has given us his very great and precious promises, so that through them you may participate in the divine nature, having escaped the corruption in the world caused by evil desires.

I can't help it. I am completely surrounded by temptation. It is uncontrollable. We live in a sinful world. Look what is on TV these days. I couldn't stop myself at one, or two, or three. He pushed me too far.

We live in a world that tries to convince us there is no escape from temptations, that we have no control over our evil desires, that everything and everyone is to blame for our actions but us. That way, when we respond out of anger, lust, frustration, or disappointment, we don't have to be accountable for our behavior because it was never our fault to begin with. But God has given us our escape through Him, and because of His very precious and real promises, we can participate in His divine nature and escape the corruption of this world. Today. He is the escape.

However, it takes a life totally committed and 100% focused on the Father. 100% of the time. No down time, no "me" time, no time apart from Him.

When we go on vacation, we don't go on vacation from Him. When we are tired, we don't let our relationship with Him fall short. He is not like a friend that we just don't call back, a picture that we take off the wall or a journal that we neglect. Whether or not we are engaged ourselves or not, He is always engaged with us. Always. Yes, the world is corrupt. The news, the images, the people, the despair, the loss, the lack of unconditional love, it is all there; and we can choose to fall into the black pit of despair, or we can choose to follow Him and escape it all. We don't have to fall victim to this world.

138

We don't. We are children of the King and with that comes eternal life for tomorrow and the daily companionship of our Father today.

Today, take responsibility for your actions. When evil comes your way (and it will), choose to see God's provisions. Choose joy amidst the storm.

Simply Love 2 Peter 1:5-7

For this very reason, make every effort to add to your faith goodness; and to goodness, knowledge; and to knowledge, self-control; and to self-control, perseverance; and to perseverance, godliness; and to godliness, mutual affection; and to mutual affection, love.

Why do we make it so hard? Start with faith and add goodness, now add knowledge, now add self-control, now add perseverance, now add godliness, now add mutual affection, now add love. He completely, completely spells it out for us. Start with your faith in Him and then add the rest. Yet, we don't follow the growth process Peter laid out. We add to it self-help books, talk shows, anything and everything to make this what we think it needs to be, trying to find a way, I am afraid, to make it a quick-fix program. In reality, there is no quick fix, and no one can do it for us.

Too often, we stop at one of these. Faith? Yes, I believe completely in God and the Bible, so I am good. But wait, of course, I should have goodness in my life: faith without works is dead. While I am living out goodness, I should continue maturing in my walk by adding knowledge. Knowledge leads right into the ability to control myself, not control my spouse, neighbors, family or friends, but myself, and not just once or twice, but all the time, which is perseverance. This is a 24/7 gig. This is all the time, every day of my life, and it is almost impossible at times. When I persevere, I gain godliness, then mutual affection, and, finally, love.

We talk about how all the world needs is love, but how do we get there? Love, real love, should be so simple, but it isn't. It isn't natural. Real love, love without agendas or passive aggression. Love untainted by this world comes only through faith, goodness, self-control, perseverance, godliness and mutual affection. God is the foundation. He loves through us. Reach deep today and follow the outline that God has given us instead of looking for something quicker, easier or shinier, for only God's direction will truly stand the test of time. God is good, my dear friends, no matter what, no matter where, He simply is. Don't let this world take that from you.

140

The Buck Stops Here 2 Peter 1:8-10

For if you possess these qualities in increasing measure, they will keep you from being ineffective and unproductive in your knowledge of our Lord Jesus Christ. But whoever does not have them is nearsighted and blind, forgetting that they have been cleansed from their past sins.

Faith, goodness, knowledge, self-control, perseverance, godliness, mutual affection and love.

If we possess these qualities in increasing measure, we will be effective and productive in our knowledge of Christ. "The buck stops here" in our responsibility to know Him better, to understand Him more, and to better impact our world. It lies with each of us. It lies with how we choose to live our lives every single day. And that is a difficult pill to swallow sometimes. It is far easier to lay the responsibility at our pastor's feet, in our youth leader's lap, or in our Sunday School teacher's hands. Our spouses aren't supportive enough, our church isn't reaching as it needs to reach, the Bible is too confusing, this music doesn't move us.

If the responsibility is ours, then during those times when we feel as if we don't understand Him or can't hear Him, it follows that we aren't being effective in our Christian walk. Instead of looking outward at what needs to be changed, we must first examine our own lives and hearts to see if along with our faith we also demonstrate goodness, knowledge, self-control, perseverance, godliness, mutual affection and love. And if we do, are we living them in increasingly good measure?

Thankfully, God offers grace and mercies anew each and every day, and allows us a fresh start when we stall out on the journey.

It Doesn't Take a Majority 2 Peter 1:11

...and you will receive a rich welcome into the eternal kingdom of our Lord and Savior Jesus Christ.

My daughter's death has deepened my faith in a way that I could never have imagined. There is no in-between. There is no gray. There is no maybe. It simply is.

This seems to penetrate all areas of my life. I find that I seek Godly wisdom, not just first, but only, for that is all that matters. The rest is just noise. It really doesn't matter if majority rules or if it is popular or the best plan. It doesn't matter at all when it is His plan.

We spend far too much time seeking when we are already there. We are literally sitting at the feet of our Savior, and we still seek the better way or our friend's path or the way that we always thought it should be.

The Kingdom is coming, and we will reach it through death or His return. I ask again, dear friends, "Are you ready?" Don't let yourself be lulled away from the reality. Again, no gray areas here, just wisdom.

Live worthy.

Accountability 2 Peter 1:12

So I will always remind you of these things, even though you know them and are firmly established in the truth you now have.

Not too long ago, it was fashionable in the church world to have an accountability partner, a friend who would ask the hard questions in order to encourage us to live Christ-filled lives. Many books were written and sermons were given about the proper way to be accountability partners. Two thousand years ago, Peter was holding fellow believers accountable, and the concept continues today.

Yet many of us continue without that inner circle or person who has our best interest in mind. We live lives devoid of that person who reminds us of Biblical truths when it looks like our foundation has weakened. The Biblical truths that don't change and can't be swayed. As the old children's song goes, "The wise man built his house upon the Rock."

Our house may literally fall apart, and all we are left clinging to is that Rock. Hurt, feeling abandoned and broken, we cling to a Rock that doesn't move. We cling to a Rock that is solid. Our accountability partners come along beside us, cheering us on, "You can do it! Cling to the Rock!"

A solid accountability partner does much more than listen to my confession. She reminds me Whose I am and what is true. She encourages me to "keep the main thing the main thing." We spend moments of grace together and remind each other that we do not walk this battle alone.

Spiritual Mirror 2 Peter 1:13-14

I think it is right to refresh your memory as long as I live in the tent of this body, because I know that I will soon put it aside, as our Lord Jesus Christ has made clear to me.

Our bodies are all that we know. They are familiar to us and we do life with them, but they do not tell the full story of who we are.

Upon seeing my daughter's body that day, I knew it was not Taellor. It wasn't. This was a body that had served her well. When her soul inhabited her body, it was strong and beautiful, but without her spirit, it was nothing more than, as Paul says, a tent. I knew my daughter well, and I knew she was not there in that body any longer.

Our world worships bodies so much. We spend time focusing on our appearance; we spend emotional energy on our tents. And, while it has been referred to as a temple, I am fearful that we spend far too much time on our outer temple upkeep and ignore the health of our soul.

The time is coming soon when our tents will be no more and all that matters is the soul. Will mine have bling but no maintenance under the hood, like a car that is decked out in fancy headlights and loud bass, but never had an oil change? It looks good and the music sounds great, but eventually it will not go anywhere. A soul without "oil" is way more costly.

Look in a spiritual mirror today, to examine the depths of who we are. Let's spend less time improving our skin and hair, and more time increasing our character.

All True 2 Peter 1:15

And I will make every effort to see that after my departure you will always be able to remember these things.

It really happened. It did.

Far too often, we read the stories in the Bible, and, even though we believe in our Lord, we place them in the same category as Greek mythology or history lessons with very little relevance for today. We latch onto faith when we need it or it serves our purpose and walk on our own two feet searching for purpose and direction the rest of the time. We know that we are to be in the world, not of it, but we keep very little distinction between the two.

Until something happens that brings us back to our knees, literally. And we remember again. We remember the strength only He can give. We remember the peace that surpasses all understanding. We remember the clarity and the gentleness with which He directs our path. We find ourselves hovering under His wings, and we find rest.

Until we garner our strength. And we forget again. We begin to press against those gentle feathers and reach beyond His covering. We bypass His strength in the hopes that ours will sustain us. We reach out, not to Him, but to the wisdom of the world. We find this world to be tangible and quick to respond. We begin to let ourselves falter in our faith journey. We reach outward instead of upward. We reach to ourselves instead of to Him. We strive for gratification instead of supplication. We work for platitudes instead of out of gratitude. We want our glory instead of His.

Until we falter again.

And quickly we run back to where the foundation is firm. We decide with all that we are not to stray far ever again. We vow not to extend past His wings of grace and into our own void. We struggle to find the reason why we ever left. We remember what we were created to be and find the strength that can move mountains and part the seas. We remember.

Satan will try to keep us from Him. He will offer us the world and all that it entails. He is a good study and recognizes our greatest weaknesses along with our treasures. He seeks to destroy all with any means possible. He lies in wait until we are either at our strongest human strength or our weakest, and then he quickly lays the snare that will entice us the most.

We mustn't forget. It is all true. How different would we live if we truly believed it all.

Live worthy.

Not Just a Story 2 Peter 1:16

For we did not follow cleverly devised stories when we told you about the coming of our Lord Jesus Christ in power, but we were eyewitnesses of his majesty.

Cleverly devised stories. I have heard so many people say that they don't know the specifics of the Bible well enough to talk to people about Jesus or to share His word. They either get caught up in the legalistic side or hung up on possibly saying something that might mess up what God is already doing in that person's life, so they hold back and say nothing at all. But truly our greatest God-story is what we have witnessed. What He has done in our lives. What He has done in our lives this week. Why do we believe? How do we know He is there? When we talk about what we have witnessed, they will see joy and the realness of our faith, not the memorization of some tract.

I'm not taking a stand against tracts; I know God can use them. I'm saying we are each living proof of His majesty. Just yesterday, my ministry schedule logistically couldn't fit into a day, let alone homeschooling Slate. God orchestrated my day. I gave it to Him, and He nailed it. Everything sailed along without a hitch. Some activities finished more quickly than usual, two meetings were combined into one. Another meeting was added to our schedule to fill our only open time slot. Our home-school curriculum was on a review day (which Slate aced, by the way). Let me just tell you what God did yesterday and does day after day after day.

Some would say this is just happenstance. Just coincidence. That God doesn't orchestrate the small things, that God has bigger things to do, that I only "see" God because I want to. Okay, I'll take the last one. I do want to see God, and I am looking for Him constantly in everything I do. I believe as I seek Him, He guides me. I want to follow Him every moment, every day of my life.

So the next time we have the opportunity to share Christ, let's share our eyewitness account about God. I think about the woman at the well, about Joshua, about the blind man, and about Lazarus. What do you think they said when someone asked them about Jesus? Do you think they even waited to be asked, or do you think they were so excited about what He had done in their lives that they gushed about their Christ?

We, too, have been given Living Water; we have seen walls fall down; we were blind, but now we see; and we have been resurrected with Christ! Let's walk around gushing about our Christ.

Live Worthy.

Quit the Rat Race 2 Peter 1:17-18

He received honor and glory from God the Father when the voice came to him from the Majestic Glory, saying, "This is my Son, whom I love; with him I am well pleased." We ourselves heard this voice that came from heaven when we were with him on the sacred mountain.

Can you imagine? Can you even imagine hearing that voice coming down from heaven as you stand on a sacred mountain with Him? Oh, my goodness. Can we imagine?

It is real, my friends. It really is. More than just words on a page, the melody of a song, or, dare I say, the topic of a well-rehearsed sermon. I am afraid we fail to live as those who believe the raw reality of it all. If we aren't careful, we lull ourselves into living week by week and day by day just trying to survive. But did He come, live and die just so we could survive?

Daily life can be a rat race. It will be a rat race if we let it. We are only in control of ourselves: our own emotions and responses. Therefore, we are accountable to the Father for the choices we make. I will stand face-to-face with God and will give a no-excuse account of my Kingdom work here or lack thereof. An account of my love here or absence of love. Being excellent at the rat race is not a point of pride in eternity.

There comes a time to step away and say, "I am done. I am done trying to live in two worlds. I am done trying to be accepted in a world that is not my home and never quite measuring up. I am done feeling guilty for not doing what I know in my heart that God has called me to do. He has called me to live differently, to be set apart, to be the light in the darkness, to be the salt of the earth. Today, I am going to focus only on Him no matter the cost."

Take time today to focus on Him through prayer, Scripture, quiet devotion time, or Christian fellowship. Saturate your soul with Him, and the desire to run the rat race will slowly fade in light of Who He is.

Reliable 2 Peter 1:19

We also have the prophetic message as something completely reliable, and you will do well to pay attention to it, as to a light shining in a dark place, until the day dawns and the morning star rises in your hearts.

Completely reliable. Not somewhat reliable.

What in our world is completely reliable? What can you depend on 100% percent of the time with no small print or disclosures?

In today's culture, there are very few, if any, absolutes. A few generations ago, a handshake or a man's word was a guarantee. Today, a "yes" can mean anything from "yes" to "maybe" to "no, but I don't want to tell you no." So we make plans, knowing that nothing is firm until it happens.

In contrast, Scripture is telling us that God's Word is completely reliable. His Word is a foundation we can be sure of no matter what. And, yet, we continue time and time again to place our trust in worldly things and people, and "wisdom" found in every place except the one place with the unshakable foundation. Then we wonder why our lives are infiltrated with false truths and advice that serves only to further the distance between us and our Creator. Eventually, God's Word becomes nothing more than a sermon to endure on Sunday morning. We regard it as a dusty book instead of the guidebook showing us how to live our lives.

Go first to His Word. Start with a Truth that is 100% reliable. His Word is black and white. It's not flashy or glamorous; but it is real, pure and solid. Isn't that what we are all searching for in this world of chaos?

Faces That Hurt 2 Peter 1:20

Above all, you must understand that no prophecy of Scripture came about by the prophet's own interpretation of things.

Today, I did something I rarely do. I took both boys at the same time to the grocery store. Now for those who regularly take multiple young kids shopping, this probably doesn't seem like much of a feat. Add in Asperger's and sensory issues, and a store where everything is in your second language, and you might see the challenge. Slaton wants to discuss everything we buy (What do we need it for? How will we cook it? Why is it packaged like that?). Antonio, who has only been in a grocery store a handful of times, still gets extremely hyper-stimulated by it, which results in strange, non-verbal sounds.

In the middle of this torturous trek through the market, I noticed Slate standing in front of his little brother, covering his head with his hands, or telling him to look in different directions. I finally reprimanded Slate pretty hard to leave his little brother alone, but he continued to bug him.

Once we got back to the car, Slate apologized, not for bugging his little brother, but for failing to keep everyone from staring at him: "Why, Mom, do they stare with faces that aren't kind? With faces that hurt?" As I turned to him with tears in my eyes, I no longer saw a big brother picking on his little brother, but a big brother, although small himself, trying to protect his little brother in the only way he knew how.

My interpretation of the situation was entirely off-base. I thought I was dealing with one over-stimulated child and one misbehaving child, but I was so far from the truth. So far.

Our human interpretations are filled with misconceptions and are biased by our own perspectives, but rest assured that the Scriptures did not come from the prophets' interpretation. Every word was inspired by the Holy Spirit.

Every precious word.

Not Just a Book 2 Peter 1:21

For prophecy never had its origin in the human will, but prophets, though human, spoke from God as they were carried along by the Holy Spirit.

God's words. How often we take them for granted.

Recently, I had the privilege of giving someone a Bible. It was a very simple, paperback Bible. Yet, tears overflowed as she embraced that Bible to her chest, because she understood it was more than just a book. It was our Father's words, as precious and holy as if they had been spoken to her in that very moment.

In many American homes, Bibles fill our shelves. We have the huge Family Bible, our kids' Bibles with their names engraved, study Bibles with footnotes galore, and our favorite Bibles with our handwritten notes beside our favorite verses. But do we hold His Word as dear? Do we daily embrace His Word with our hearts, or do we only carry it to church on Sundays?

Scholars and cynics tell us the Bible is a mere book, and that it has many mistakes and flaws. They tell us that men wrote each word, so it must be wrong.

But this so-called "book" contains much more than a historical account. It is filled with God's inspired words, each and every one detailing advice to His children. This is how you live, this is how you walk, this is how you love. It is just as relevant today as it was when it was written.

When was the last time you held your Bible so close you could feel the indentions on your arms? When did you last feel tears flowing in response to His holiness as you read His words? Have you given a Bible to someone else, sharing words of life with the nations?

Be on Guard 2 Peter 2:1

But there were also false prophets among the people, just as there will be false teachers among you. They will secretly introduce destructive heresies, even denying the sovereign Lord who brought them-bringing swift destruction on themselves.

We have one God. One Truth. Period.

Anything you hear or read must be carefully evaluated against Scripture. Does it contradict? Does it blur the lines?

Be on guard. We have been warned that false teachers exist. What concerns me most is that they secretively introduce these false ideas in a direct affront against Christ and His followers. Intentionally, they weave lies, cause distrust and seek to cause man to turn away from God. Not inadvertently or accidentally. Intentionally.

As believers, we must know the Truth so that we are not swayed like branches in the wind. When God's Word and Who He is comes under attack, we will be ready to speak the Truth to defend Him. Even though our society seems to have embraced an "any idea is valid" or "anything goes" philosophy, this is not Truth. It isn't. And it sure isn't popular to say it isn't.

We must live in such a way that over time, those who have intentionally woven lies into the cultural worldview will see that we believe in a Truth that is unchanging and unmodified. As satan's lies become exposed for what they are, those who once criticized our God will search for Him. Let us be a people who extends mercy and grace.

"For our struggle is not against flesh and blood, but against the rulers, against the authorities, against the powers of this dark world and against the spiritual forces of evil in the heavenly realms" (Ephesians 6:12).

This is not paranoia. This is readiness. He warned us so we would not be blindsided. Let's be ready.

The True Battle 2 Peter 2:2

Many will follow their depraved conduct and will bring the way of truth into disrepute.

Not a few, not some, but many will follow. Those who do not follow will be under scrutiny, and some will be discredited, and this character assault will distract from the Truth. That's the main purpose, yes? Not to discredit us as believers or to hurt us personally. No, remember, this is not a battle against flesh and blood. If that's all it was, the purpose of their depraved conduct would be to hurt our feelings, stir up emotions and kill relationships. But it isn't about that; it isn't about us. It is about the Truth and God's Kingdom.

These are battles for souls, and they have eternal repercussions. Even the evil walking among us realizes that this world is not our home. We think that it is about us. We think that it is personal, but we are just part of the diversion. We are just pawns, if we allow ourselves to be. Pawns that cause distraction or doubt in seekers' minds, which will keep them from continuing to seek the Truth. If we allow ourselves to be caught up in the battle being fought, then we become part of the smoke screen that keeps others from the Truth.

Does it hurt our feelings to be called names? Yes. Does it hurt our feelings to be spoken against? Absolutely. But does it matter? Do our feelings really matter? They shouldn't. We have been told that the journey on this earth would be difficult. Look at Christ's example here on earth. Yes, He taught us to love freely, but He also showed us what it would be like to be betrayed, hated and ultimately put to death. His was not an easy journey, but he walked it in such a way that even those who put Him to death could find no blame. They were not given the satisfaction of Him retaliating or diverting others from the Truth.

I have been guilty of jumping into the battle. One time, years ago, I had been treated badly, and I began to return the hateful treatment. Yes, I knew what I was saying was wrong, but, oh, how she had hurt me. I remember on one particularly bad night, I was about to respond in a harsh way, and my husband gently said, "Does this bring glory to His Kingdom or to your pride?"

 If he hadn't said it gently, I wouldn't have listened. I knew he was speaking words of wisdom, and I knew he was right. Although it would have felt amazing and she deserved it, it would have been wrong, and it would have distracted others from my Father's Kingdom.

Even when we are in the midst of turmoil, we are called to be Light in the dark world. Always.

The One I Serve 2 Peter 2:3

In their greed these teachers will exploit you with stories they have made up. Their condemnation has long been hanging over them, and their destruction has not been sleeping.

While teaching Sunday School during my early years as a Christian with one amazing teacher, I heard over and over again her telling our third graders concerning the Bible not to take anything that anyone said at face value, not to watch any movie about God's word and call it Truth without reading that portion in the Bible ourselves to verify.

There are many false teachers. Beware.

They have been tempted by an increase of money, power, pride or fill in the blank. Greed, a very present desire for payment in the here and now. A payment that comes with the intent to divert those seeking Truth.

Of course, it isn't spelled out like that. Satan doesn't tempt us with full disclosures. (Here is the opportunity for you to speak with all authority of God but instead of saying all of the Truth, only use the parts about happiness and fulfillment. This will increase your membership greatly.) or (Yes, the Bible does say only one way but that can be taken to mean really so many ways.) or (Of course we are all Christians. We all believe in God and we ultimately all believe in Jesus Christ. Our positions on His authority may be a little different.). I've heard each one of these at one time or another and while to some they may seem unbelievable and to others they might seem not so bad they each cause distraction to God's Word and muddy up the Truth.

If satan had to offer a full disclosure in your life what would it be? We can look upon the words "false teachers" in disgust but where do we fall short in bringing full glory to God's Word? Yes, there are those with the intent to seek and destroy but there are also those of us who unintentionally muddy God's Word. This is the part that we can control. We can live such a life, such a testimony to our Christ, that false teachers would be highlighted by the vast differences of our actions.

Live different.

No Favorites 2 Peter 2:4

For if God did not spare angels when they sinned, but sent them to hell, putting them in chains of darkness to be held for judgment;

God is just. He doesn't play favorites. No one will slide by, and no one can con or sweet talk Him.

It is quite simple actually. Do you believe that He is your Savior? Do you understand that we are all sinners who can only be cleansed through His blood? Do you wish to follow Him? That's it. It is a decision that can be made in the largest church by walking down an aisle or at home by responding to God alone. What follows next is astounding: transformation. We are new creations; God makes us into the beautiful masterpieces He had in mind at Creation. He effects a heart change, a life change.

Tae's death taught me many things, but the greatest lesson so far has been the awesomeness of God. She was here fully engaged in this world, and a moment later, she was gone. Gone from this world. Gone. We could argue all day and night that she was too young, that she was doing incredible things for His Kingdom, selflessly living for Him, and yet, when her time came, regardless what she was doing, He called her home. Wow. I have seen God's work, but to experience His mighty power that takes life from this world left me speechless.

I read Scripture differently now. In the past, when I read about the parting of the seas or a day being longer than the rest, I questioned, "How? But after experiencing God's power on that afternoon in June, I have learned that God can do anything. Yes, it's an elementary principle, but do we really live it? From that moment on, I will.

When the awesomeness of God comes to you, will you be ready? Will it be a day of celebration or a day of judgment? There is no jury. Only One. One Way. One Truth.

Found Worthy 2 Peter 2:5

If He did not spare the ancient world when He brought the flood on its ungodly people, but protected Noah, a preacher of righteousness, and seven others . . .

Let us be like Noah. When every other person on earth is living a godless existence, let us remain steadfast and true.

Back when our older kids were teenagers, they did not fit the mold. I remember the time I encouraged them to be part of the crowd, to join in and be friends with the group. I will never forget when they both turned to ask me, "Do you really want that? Do you want us to be part of a crowd that pretends to be one way when parents are around and another when they leave? Do you want that?"

I realized they were taking a stand about who they were, but also Whose they were. They were choosing to live differently, in the world and not of it, and I, their mother, had almost missed the whole thing. Just like the days of Noah, there isn't a middle ground here. There isn't. We can't belong to both the world and God. Sometimes that means stepping away from the world. Sometimes that means being criticized and labeled as judgmental and narrow-minded. Sometimes that means not doing what the crowd does, but staying the course, following Christ and Christ alone.

There are those who believe that God is too loving of a God to bring His last judgment on this earth. I wonder how many drops of rain fell, how high the water had to climb for the people outside the boat to realize this was real.

Don't wait outside the boat with the crowd. Live in such a way that your every action reflects Christ and Christ alone.

He is God 2 Peter 2:6

[I]f He condemned the cities of Sodom and Gomorrah by burning them to ashes, and made them an example of what is going to happen to the ungodly . . .

I was asked recently about the place in Joshua where God kept the sun from setting until the battle was won. What did I think of this? Did I believe it? Maybe God didn't mean it literally, "for we all know through science that this is impossible," so maybe it only meant the sun seemed not to set.

Through the events surrounding Tae's death, I have experienced God in a way I never have before. I have seen things I would have deemed unbelievable if I hadn't experienced them first-hand. Unbelievable, not possible by the confines of this earth, but they happened. God can do anything. Anything that He wants. Anything.

Why aren't we okay with that? Why can't we accept that He is who He is and rest on that? Why do we have a difficult time sharing with others the parts of our faith that are just that: Faith. Not explainable in the earthly realm. The night that Tae died, I took out my contact lenses, knowing I would have difficulty seeing due to the tears. The next morning, I awoke to a blurry world, of course, both literally and figuratively. However, later that morning as Trav and I sat outside praying and crying out to our Father, I looked up and saw with the most amazing crispness the mountains in the far distance, each and every leaf on the trees, single strands of grass in the most vivid color beyond my imagination.

For the next three days, when I would find myself falling into despair, my eyes would literally be opened to almost another world. When I drove into the village for her funeral, as tears started to cloud my eyes, I found I could see beyond what I have ever seen before even with my contacts. Vivid colors were all around. Unexplainable? It doesn't matter to me how it happened. He did it. At a time when I needed clarity the most, He simply provided beyond measure.

Sodom and Gomorrah was meant to be more than just a lesson to the people who watched the destruction first-hand. Because it was included in the Bible, this is a lesson to us all. We can choose to "intellectually" dismiss it, but that doesn't mean it didn't happen and that the lesson wasn't for each one of us. The Master of all teachers has spoken. Now it is our turn to respond.

Lawlessness 2 Peter 2:7-8

[A]nd if He rescued Lot, a righteous man, who was distressed by the depraved conduct of the lawless (for that righteous man, living among them day after day, was tormented in his righteous soul by the lawless deeds he saw and heard) . . .

We aren't the first.

We aren't the first to encounter a lawless world. A world filled with hate, darkness, pettiness and overall despair. We aren't. The Bible is filled with real accounts of obedient people living in a world spiraling out of control. A world that appeared to be ripping apart at the seams. And in each one of these accounts, God remained completely in control. God took care of those who maintained a righteous life.

Sometimes we wonder, "Where is God in all of this? How can we continue on as we are?" We forget that the One who created us is fully engaged during every moment of our lives, or we seek to fix things, or we give in or give up, or we use it as an excuse to join the world. God doesn't change. He is constant. His foundation stays equally firm in the Garden of Eden and in a land filled with hedonism. Truth is not variable. If we are not careful, we find ourselves emulating the world. Listening when we know we shouldn't, speaking words that do not build up others, sitting back when we know we should stand, we find ourselves adrift. Saved but not strong. Redeemed but not direct reflections of our Christ.

I pray that when God looks upon this world, He doesn't have to look far to see Truth reflected. To the outside world, we may act and look different; we may stand apart by choosing to go to church on Sunday and attend Christian events, but how do we look to God? Are we a true reflection of our Christ? I know, I know, it seems to be an almost insurmountable task, right? We give ourselves excuses and the permission to be less than. We live a life steeped in grace and mercy but with very little discipline. But there have always been, and there always will be, the faithful ones God sees when He looks the world over.

What will God see when His gaze falls upon you and your life? Will He find a life lived for Him or a life lived for the world?

No Greater Justice 2 Peter 2:9

[I]f this is so, then the Lord knows how to rescue the godly from trials and to hold the unrighteous for punishment on the day of judgment.

Justice will be done. Rest assured.

I used to struggle greatly with the "principles of the matter," the injustices of the world, the hollow truths and empty promises. Then I found Christ, who holds the unrighteous accountable. Christ, who will ultimately right all of the wrongs. Every knee will bow. Christ who is just and fair. It's his job to judge, not mine. There are many things in this world that I simply do not understand. Yet, I have learned to rest quietly in the One who does. I don't have to know every second of every day, every detail in every event, because He does, and He works all things together for my good. But to do this, to rest quietly in the One who saves us all, I have to trust in a way I've never trusted before. I have to trust fully with every fiber of my being that He is everything He says He is.

Do I?

Can I?

When the world crashes around me, when the back-story isn't what it appears to be, when I'm confronted with blatant deception, when my own daughter dies from a fall in a hammock, do I trust Him enough to know that He will judge appropriately and fairly? Can I simply lay it all at the cross and walk away, knowing that He will do what needs to be done? Walk away, knowing that He knows infinitely more than I. Walk away, knowing that He loves us all, even the accused. Walk away and quit trying to fulfill God's role as Judge. It's natural for me to meddle, because I truthfully want to make sure that it gets done right, as if I could ever know more than Him. Lay it at the cross and walk away.

There is freedom here. Great freedom, if we can bypass the thoughts of the world and lay it all at the Cross.

His Authority 2 Peter 2:10

This is especially true of those who follow the corrupt desire of the flesh and despise authority.

Authority.

We live in a world full of people who struggle to respect authority figures: parents, bosses, teachers or even well-meaning friends. We really don't want anyone in our business, especially when it gets personal.

Self-made men and women. We've created a society where we don't need anyone but ourselves, where we can't count on anyone but ourselves, and God tends to be the ultimate authority figure we rebel against.

Satan has woven lies in such a way that, if we are not careful, we begin to believe we don't need anyone at all telling us what to do. We are our own authorities. No one has the right to tell us what to do, especially an "old book." But that is the stone that will trip us, for this "old book" is more than just mere words, it's a living masterpiece. And God, as our Creator, is our authority, whether we wish to be obedient or not. He is Who He is with or without our agreement. Our belief isn't what makes Him God. He simply is.

When God calls us to obedience, do we follow? Do we follow joyfully so that our very obedience is a testimony to Him, or do we follow begrudgingly, complaining to all who will listen? The One who knows us best, the One who wants the very best for us is the One who has true Authority over us, and that should bring us comfort always.

Bold and arrogant, they are not afraid to heap abuse on celestial beings; yet even angels, although they are stronger and more powerful, do not heap abuse on such beings when bringing judgment on them from the Lord.

And who are we? We are children of the King. We are children of the Almighty. Sisters and brothers in Christ. We are not the King, not the Almighty, not the Christ. We simply are not. Yet, we yearn to be so. We yearn to be the one people look up to. We yearn to be the one others turn to for answers and for direction. We yearn to be the person in charge. We yearn to be the person who aligns our own universe. Boldly and arrogantly, we act as if we are, and then when something happens that reminds us we are not, we get upset and we turn on the very Creator. We assume we are being treated unjustly.

During our third month in Nicaragua, Taellor was becoming overwhelmed by the poverty. The requests for basic needs never ended, things such as food, water and medicine. It's a never-ending cycle. There is never, ever enough. I shared with her that I, too, once struggled with it, and then I asked her what it would look like if we did have enough for everyone. What if we had enough food for everyone who asked, the exact medicines they needed every single time, and shoes and clothes for all who wanted them. Who would they begin to look for if they had a need? Would they pray first? Would they look toward Christ or would they look for us?

Our purpose here is to point them toward the One who can save us all. The One who can provide all of our needs, before we even realize they are needs. He is also the One who knows what we need to lead us to Him. Sometimes, we need an empty stomach or shoeless feet. Sometimes, instead of temporarily numbing that ache with worldly provisions, we need a long period of need. He extends in His infinite wisdom exactly what will guide us to spiritual maturity. And yet we fight this kicking and screaming, sometimes.

Sometimes we barter with Him, begging Him to just answer this one, and then we will obey, but He, unlike our friends, can see into our very souls. He knows what we need, even when we do not. Being children of the King is a grand privilege that comes with even greater responsibility. We are to be willing to be fully His. Always, every day. Who are we to judge Him?

164

Personal Gain 2 Peter 2:12

But these men blaspheme in matters they do not understand. They are like unreasoning animals, creatures of instinct, born only to be caught and destroyed, and like animals they too will perish.

Scripture is brutally clear about those who use God's word for their gain, those who twist the Truth until it is a bleak resemblance of what it actually is.

For this very Truth that they twist is real. It is. Do they not realize the depth of its realness? Do they not realize the magnitude of our Father's power or His wrath?

They claim to be His followers. They claim they are representing His words, but they are masqueraders, blending Truth with the world. Outwardly, they initially appear to be glowing representations of God's Word, until the pageantry turns into work and the superficial nature of their character is revealed.

Yes, in this dark world, they are encouraged and rewarded for their behavior. Sadly, they are blinded and deceived by the very one who seeks to destroy us all.

The game, so to speak, is real. We must be as cautious about aligning ourselves with blasphemers as they were when this Scripture was written. We must constantly be on-guard, search Scriptures and be mindful of the Holy Spirit's discernment.

Smooth-talkers may seem to conquer this world, but their mastery of manipulation will have no value in eternity. They may seem to have it all, but it is all smoke and mirrors, just like the wizard in the Land of Oz.

Be Ready 2 Peter 2:13

They will be paid back with harm for the harm they have done. Their idea of pleasure is to carouse in broad daylight. They are blots and blemishes, reveling in their pleasures while they feast with you.

They boldly deny Jesus; they flaunt their hedonism, guiltless and flamboyant.

In broad daylight? Feast with you? These descriptions are not what I would use to paint a picture of those seeking to destroy God's kingdom. I would prefer them to look like they do in horror films: dark and ghoulish, accompanied by haunting music. These folks seem to be well-intentioned, maybe even fun. They may be trusted mentors, family members or friends. They make their way into our world feasting at our table and taking pleasure in our anticipated fall.

Too paranoid? Too pessimistic? God's Word tells us this is how they will be. How should we respond? We naturally want to reconcile the carousers in our world with the pretty picture we see in our heads. We struggle to change ourselves to try to appease them as they revel in our discomfort.

Instead, we need a reality check. Although we are always called to love, we must set boundaries to prevent them from ruining our faith.

Building the Foundation 2 Peter 2:14

With eyes full of adultery, they never stop sinning; they seduce the unstable; they are experts in greed-an accursed brood!

Peter continues to warn us of false teachers, "an accursed brood." They seduce the unstable.

What is our foundation? Our quick response will surely be, "God is my firm foundation." We've all built our house on the rock. Not sinking sand, yes? But have we really?

This is not a one time, "fire-insurance" policy. A walk down the aisle, a prayer with hugs and handshakes. It is not. Our salvation is just the beginning; our foundation is laid during each moment spent with our Savior, through prayers spoken, Scriptures read, sermons studied, obedience enacted.

What if you were to find out a war is coming, and you have one year to prepare to personally defend your life and your family. What would you do? You would prepare. You would train. You would acquire all you might need to succeed. You would learn all you could about your opponent and what his weakness might be.

We are already in a battle. Our opponent is the greatest of all seducers, and he never stops. Never stops. Are we preparing? Do we let precious moments slip away that might have been used to firm up our shores? Do we put our heads in the sand, assuming it's too late; we've already been noticed, spied on and engaged.

The response is ours alone. The wisest soldier will arm himself with spiritual armor and battle close to God. Just as the branches are most stable closest to the trunk, we are strongest when we are closely connected to Him. The ignorant soldier will run into battle without his God-armor and will forget to stay close to the Leader. Unprepared and far out on a limb, he will fall prey to the seduction of the evil one.

167

Pray, dear ones. Read your Bible daily. It isn't optional in this life. Prepare, and battle close to God.

Warning 2 Peter 2:15

They have left the straight way and wandered off to follow the way of Balaam, son of Bezer, who loved the wages of wickedness.

They left the straight way.

A warning to us all. Balaam was hired by a pagan king to curse Israel. Initially, he did as God told him to do. He followed God's commands. He was obedient. Over time, though, his evil motives and desires became more important than his obedience to God, and he began to use his relationship with God as a means to advance himself personally. Instead of a personal relationship with God, he turned to religion and used it.

Nothing that we have done through God's hand has been done by our human strength, and yet, if we are not careful, we find ourselves in the same predicament as Balaam with satan laying the same lies at our feet: "Look what you have done. Look what you have built. You have managed a company, a corporation, a nation. Single-handedly. Without you, none of this would have been possible. Without you, it would all fall."

And, ever so slowly, if we aren't clinging daily to God, who exposes satan's lies for what they are, we start to believe that we did this. We organized the best Bible study group, we fed the poor, we formed a ministry that has saved millions. We did it. Our eyes are blinded to the many people, places and things God placed in our path to make us successful. We take the first step off the straight path and begin to walk down a road that will eventually end in despair and destruction. The golden road will decay, and we will see that it wasn't us at all.

It is easy to see those who have stepped off the straight path. It is easy to point fingers and shake heads. To see my own misdirection is more difficult.

Today, let's ask God to show us how we have wandered, and to help us stay on the straight path.

Identity 2 Peter 2:16

But he was rebuked for his wrongdoing by a donkey-an animal without speech-who spoke with a human voice and restrained the prophet's madness.

We could learn a lot from Balaam. He wasn't one of God's chosen, but he acknowledged God as powerful. He used obedience as a tool for his gain, and it ultimately led to his destruction. A man of many facades and many masks. A man who could appear to be anything with anyone, given the correct circumstances.

At work, school, home, a dinner party, a mission trip, a class reunion, who are we?

Do we look at our lives and see who God created us to be, or who we wish we could be? Who we wish the world could see us as?

Why can't they be one and the same?

God sees all of our masks for what they truly are, an ill attempt to be accepted. He sees the facades we create in order to find inclusion and approval from this world. In this world that is not our home, we will never find true acceptance. Never. So the facades continue as we try to find just the right look, the right voice, the right house, the right spouse, the right car, job, school, clothes, etc., and the madness continues.

Yet God waits. He waits for us to turn directly to Him and say, "Enough." He waits for us to realize the Truth: that satan does lie and this is all for naught. He waits for our hearts to be ready to embrace Him and what He wants to do with our lives. And when we are ready, He takes our lives and radically changes them in a way that is totally unrecognizable by this world and yet more beautiful and fulfilling than we could ever imagine.

He sets us free.

No more worrying about being seen for who we really are inside. He takes our scared, timid selves and brings out the true awesomeness of His creation. No more despair and lust over what we cannot have. He takes our very souls and fills them with His desires and love so much so that they overflow into love for others. No more craziness in our minds as we try to dissect every conversation we have in order to reply in just the right manner. He shapes our mind so that we become more like Him, and we strive to build up others instead of plotting their destruction so we might succeed. If we step aside, truly aside and not just when it suits us, He brings out the true wonder of His creation.

Drop the masks today. Find life as it was truly meant to be.

Stand Ready 2 Peter 2:17

These men are springs without water and mists driven by a storm. Blackest darkness is reserved for them.

If only they appeared as visibly dried up men and women with sunken skin and cracked lips, we might not fall prey. If only a visible cloud of black mist hung over their heads, we might walk away.

They appear as friends, mentors, colleagues, co-workers and relatives. Their dry spirits express themselves with dirty looks, backstabbing gossip, twisted lies and deceit. Sometimes it seems as if we are the only ones who see the evil that spews forth. God's Word is Truth. He offers us promises of grace and mercy, but He also tells us that He will deal with the unjust. It is tempting to fall to our own devices. It is tempting to betray as we are betrayed. It is tempting to lash out at those who have lashed out at us, but our task at hand is to shine Christ's Light. Our task is to be obedient and love. We've been warned time and time again to stand guard and be ready.

Be ready. It hurts, dear ones. It will seem to break our hearts and threaten to take away our joy. But our joy is found in Him, not them. Always.

172

Betrayal 2 Peter 2:18

For they mouth empty, boastful words and, by appealing to the lustful desires of the flesh, they entice people who are just escaping from those who live in error.

Recently, I reflected about who I was twenty years ago, and I gave praises to God for the wisdom He has given me since then. Early in my career, I thought it was best to hide my Light, and display it only behind closed doors and when asked. During those times, the voices that offered emptiness and chaos were louder than His, so I listened.

I sought guidance in mentors, in professors, in teachers and in older women. I sought guidance from those the world would deem extremely successful, and, through them, I, too, found success by worldly measures. I found deadlines met and results obtained, but they were ultimately overshadowed by emptiness and chaos. I also found pride, self-promotion and fear of betrayal.

My fear of betrayal was ultimately justified. And through the darkness of that betrayal, I found the One who teaches servant leadership by giving it all for us. Realizing I could not count on the loyalty of those around me, I began to lean on Christ alone. His wisdom directed me to develop parameters for my inner circle. I found that people who quickly befriend and offer advice aren't always the ones I should trust. And that financial and professional success does not necessarily reflect good character. I learned that what mattered most in mentors is their relationship with Christ, the fruits of their lives and where their treasures are laid.

Growing in wisdom didn't come easy; this is wisdom that comes only by living life and learning from it. Wisdom imparted by making mistakes and finally realizing it was in Him where I would find true Guidance.

Praising the Father today of second chances who offers hope to us all.

Lift our voices. Speak in kindness. Speak in love.

Never Forgotten 2 Peter 2:19

They promise them freedom, while they themselves are slaves of depravity-for "people are slaves to whatever has mastered them."

Promises of freedom. Promises of a better life. Promises of the land of milk and honey. Promises of grandeur. Empty promises.

I have the privilege of serving hundreds of ladies and girls each week. The ladies and girls who are working in the sex trade stepped into that arena with promises of a better lot in life. Promises of something beyond what they currently see. Quickly, whatever self-respect and confidence they might have had is stripped away, and the promises are revealed for what they are—lies.

And those who had enticed them are revealed for what they truly are.

Left alone, they slowly lose as the reality of the situation takes root deep within their souls.

Yet, we serve a God who sees hope in the darkest places of the world. We serve a God who believes in second chances and who holds the poorest of the poor in greatest esteem. And our God forgets no one.

The world is full of empty promises of freedom. Lose weight, live in this neighborhood, drive this car, go to this church and sit in this pew and find freedom. We quickly find that the freedom is short-lived and comes with snarls and conditions that enslave us until our "freedom" isn't really freedom at all, and we find ourselves entrapped in a deep pit.

Slowly, we lose sight of who we are. We initially expect our character to be enhanced; instead, it's diminished. We think our true beauty will shine; instead, it fades. We become more limited by our surroundings until we are a mere resemblance of who we once were, and then we are told we no longer have value and are cast aside alone.

If you find yourself here, call out to the only One who can restore you to who you once were. With gentle hands, with the soft touch of a feather's wings, He will guard and protect your soul.

Say, "Help me." And He will be there.

To Know 2 Peter 2:20

If they have escaped the corruption of the world by knowing our Lord and Savior Jesus Christ and are again entangled in it and are overcome, they are worse off at the end than they were at the beginning.

They are worse off at the end than they were at the beginning.

In the beginning, they simply didn't know. They didn't know who Christ was, what His gift of salvation offers or how depraved their deeds were. They didn't know. They hadn't yet been positively influenced by Christians or loved unconditionally. Ever. They didn't know that there was a true lifeline that could reach deep into the furthest depths and pull, even them, from the certainty of death. They didn't know that the promises written in the Bible and the blood that was shed on the cross were for them, too.

Until they did know.

Some moments define us; they change us forever. The moment when you fall in love, the moment when you experience death head-on, the moment when you first believe. Before and after. No turning back, for to turn back would be to try to place yourself back into a place that no longer exists. We now know and can never "un-know." We now know what it is like to be in love, what it is like to lose a loved one, what it is like to be touched by the Father, and we can't go back to where we were before. We can try. We can try to pretend not to know. We can run far away and hide in the shadows, but, hidden away from the prying eyes of the world, deep down, we still know.

We know we have experienced Truth. We walked down an aisle and said, "I do." We raised our hands and repeated a few words. In our heart of hearts, though, we held something back. Pride, perhaps? Fear of losing control? Peer pressure? For whatever reason, we find ourselves refusing to grab the only lifeline that can truly save us.

So we sway back and forth. When we feel abandoned by this world, we run to God. When we feel let down by this world, we run to God. When we are hurt, rejected, unloved, or mistreated, we run back to the place that we know.

176

Yet, when the world's praise and chaos fills our minds, we never acknowledge the Hand that held us and ignore the emptiness inside.

For those of us who know Him, we must believe in Him. It is not enough to know His name, it is not enough to go to church, tithe or call ourselves His. This world will tell you it is. But, we can only serve one master. Only one. One will fight for your soul with deceit and lies. The other has already died on the cross for you so you can live. It is a choice. It simply is.

To Know 2 Peter 2:21

It would have been better for them not to have known the way of righteousness, than to have known it and then to turn their backs on the sacred command that was passed on to them.

It would have been better for them not to have known.

The rich young ruler knew who Christ was. He knew who He was, yet he wasn't able to give all that Christ required. We are told that the demons know His reputation well enough to shudder in fear. We are also told of a lady whose simple faith led her to believe that touching the hem of His cloak would heal her. She pressed through the crowds to touch his cloak, and she was immediately healed. Just a touch.

Where do we fit in?

Do we know enough of Him to keep His commandments, yet are unwilling to surrender fully? Do we know enough about Him to fear Him, yet, for whatever reason, we give our very souls to satan? Or do we believe in Who He is, knowing that a touch from Him can heal us.

Satan will whisper in your ear that you don't need to give your all. You don't really have to surrender everything, for to do so would be considered radical, and that is just plain crazy. Go with the crowd. Blend in. Don't reach out too much, too far. For what if it isn't true? And so on and on he goes, weaving his lies of doubt, causing seekers to stumble and believers to be ineffective.

I strive to be like the lady who didn't mind the crowd. Perhaps in her quest to touch the One she knew could heal her, she didn't even see them. Her belief was so strong and pure that even satan's lies couldn't penetrate it. If that is considered radical, so be it.

I'm sure there were many who thought Abraham was radical to leave his homeland and Sarah was justified in taking matters into her own hands. I'm sure there were many who ridiculed Noah and mocked Moses and praised the Pharisees.

The day will come when knowing will be synonymous with believing. Every knee will bow, but not all will be called His.

Free Will 2 Peter 2:22

Of them the proverbs are true: "A dog returns to its vomit," and, "A sow that is washed returns to her wallowing in the mud."

Free will. The freedom to choose where we shall place our allegiance. The freedom, or so it seems, to move back and forth from cleansed to dirty, then back again to cleansed. But does this really represent freedom? Can it be truly defined as freedom when we are held so captive to our old ways that we continue to find ourselves back where we were before, not maturing, cycling in a round of despair and happiness and taking as many casualties with us as we can.

Today's world glorifies free will. Commends those who choose differently. Encourages those who walk their own path as long as that choice and that path leads away from God. As long as the free will is exercised to break away from the One who created us, the One who loved us enough to give us free will.

Loved us enough to give us free will so that we would not be robots, that we would choose Him over evil, that we would choose life over death.

Instead, we find ourselves choosing complacency over choice. We find ourselves busily running through our days and exercising our free will. We fill up our lives with all that this world offers, little of which will follow us into eternity. Yes, He sends us encouragement and guidance along the way, and we feel a spike in our spiritual life; but then the next deadline comes upon us, the next event, the next program, or the next love. The spike becomes a distant memory of what we could experience every day.

We say we want faith like Abraham or experiences like David and Noah. We say we want to experience God as He was recorded in the Bible. They all chose to exercise their free will to follow Him. How can we assume that we could experience even a portion of His goodness when we use our free will to follow everything but Him?

Live worthy.

A Choice 2 Peter 3:1

Dear friends, this is now my second letter to you. I have written both of them as reminders to stimulate you to wholesome thinking.

Whew! And this is how we shall live.

It amazes me how Peter's letters are as relevant today as they were to the very churches who received them. A world filled with contradictory messages and a widespread rejection of Truth. A world voicing its desire for Truth while striving for individual gain regardless of others' loss.

Peter reminds us time and time again where our focus as believers should be. He reminds us how we should live. He reminds us that we should expect an attack around every corner. Peaceful calm is the exception when you are following His will. As we examine our own lives, let's ask these questions: How do our lives reflect His Light? When the time comes for us to depart from this world, will there be a void? Will our church family be disabled because our spiritual gifts are missing? Will our Bibles, creased and worn, be lonely? Will the people we served remember what we taught them? Will we have pointed them toward Christ?

I remember when my grandmother passed away, I lost the one person in this world who prayed for me personally without failing. My name. Every single day, at least once. When Tae passed, it was her servant's heart to the poorest of the poor I missed the most. Both of them were true reflections of Christ.

As I look upon my own reflection, I am challenged to let go of the noise in this world, the craziness, the negativity and anything that might take away from His Light shining its brightest.

The Lies 2 Peter 3:2

I want you to recall the words spoken in the past by the holy prophets and the command given by our Lord and Savior through your apostles.

Satan lies.

He does. He will twist, deceive, mock and manipulate in such a manner that sometimes even the most faithful may pause to wonder and to question. He did it to Eve in the Garden of Eden. Why wouldn't he do it now? Did God really say that? Are you certain? What if there is more than one way? What about this interpretation? Maybe you simply misunderstood, misheard, misinterpreted.

No, satan, you are simply wrong. Wrong.

There is a Truth. One Truth. One Way. One God. I didn't misunderstand, mishear nor misinterpret. I know what I know and that God is who He says He is. The Bible is Truth, and there is no compromise.

And this is faith. Faith that will stand when held to a flame. Faith that will endure. Faith that will not sway relative to public opinion. True faith.

Remember what you have been taught. God is the great I Am. He simply is. The God of Abraham, Isaac and Jacob. The same today as He was then and as He will be tomorrow. When doubt slips into your mind, go back to what you know.

Sit at His feet and remember Who He is.

Don't Be Surprised 2 Peter 3:3

Above all, you must understand that in the last days scoffers will come, scoffing and following their own evil desires.

Above all.

Is there anything else? He tells us, above all, expect that there will be those who will not only reject Christ but will also mock, ridicule and make fun of us for our faith. Toward the end of this time on earth, there will be those who openly jeer and put down where we place our hope. They will continue in their worldly ways, and they will not leave us alone to stand in our faith. They will make sport of our beliefs. Of Truth.

When I first became a believer, I so badly wanted everyone, everyone to believe. I would try to fashion just the right words, the right moment and the right place so they might believe as if their very souls rested on my preparation. I have since realized that it is Christ who draws them to Himself through the Holy Spirit. His Presence, not mine. My part is to be obedient to my portion of the call. That's it. With discernment and my daily walk as a testimony, I obey His direction, and the rest is up to them. Not me.

Some will listen politely and shake their heads no. Some will yell obscenities and walk away. Some, with tears streaming down their faces, shake their heads and turn away. And some, those whose harvest time has come, will say, "Yes!" We tend to think that the "yes's" are the only important part, and the "no's" are wasted time and energy, but for each time of rejection, a seed has been planted. A tiny thought has taken root, and, at the Holy Spirit's prompting, it may continue to grow.

So, scoffers, scoff. Disbelievers, ridicule. I answer to the Lord Most High. Above all.

Attention Scoffers 2 Peter 3:4

They will say, "Where is this 'coming' he promised? Ever since our ancestors died, everything goes on as it has since the beginning of creation."

And the scoffers scoff.

Imagine that feeling you get in the pit of your stomach when you can't quite buy into a possibility. Yet, the nagging feeling of truth never quite goes away, and that something becomes reality. I imagine that feeling was felt by the scoffers at the cross, and, I'm afraid, will be felt with the same magnitude when Christ returns.

Can you imagine the scoffers who stood at the foot of the cross on which Christ was crucified? They mocked Him, only to experience at the moment of His final breath the wonders of God firsthand: the darkness, the curtain ripping in the temple, an earthquake and dead people rising from their tombs.

And when they saw all that had happened, they were terrified and exclaimed, "Surely, He was the Son of God!" Wow.

We will be surrounded by scoffers. There will be scoffers who just straight-out tell us we are crazy, a radical bunch of people wasting our lives on a good man and a book. There will be scoffers who are more politically correct, and with "kindness," they mock our literal belief in creation and the resurrection. There will be scoffers who point out the exclusivity of believing there is only one way. And the mockers will mock and the scoffers will scoff.

I imagine the scene at the cross was a preview of the scene that will play out when Christ returns. The scoffers will still be mocking the King of Kings, and then, in a blink of an eye, Christ will return: "Surely, He is the Son of God."

Deliberately Forget 2 Peter 3:5

But they deliberately forget that long ago by God's word the heavens came into being and the earth was formed out of water and by water.

They deliberately forget.

Do we deliberately forget? I know we tend to think it would be easier to believe if we lived in the days of Jesus. If we could have seen Jesus' hands at work, miracles like water turned into wine and the blind man seeing, then we could have this undeniable, unquestionable faith. And yet, I wonder, if we had lived in that day, would we have given another excuse, like we would have undeniable, unquestionable, incredible faith if we only had a clear explanation of God in the written Word. We could believe if we had the history behind it all.

Remember, there were very few who actually believed even though they walked and talked with the Living King face-to-face. And yet, today, we experience the Holy Spirit in a way that Jesus described we would. We see Him active in our lives. Intimately involved. We see God's creation surrounding us. We have His Word that gives us the history along with His commentary, Jesus' very own commentary. We see the blind seeing, the sick healed. Miracles surround us daily. Daily. And yet, we deliberately forget.

Until we remember. Until something happens that reminds us, "Oh yeah, this world is not my home." Maybe an unexpected blessing, an unexpected hardship. Anything that reminds us that we are not the center of the universe. This is not about us. Our center is brought back to balance and we turn face-on to Christ. Until we forget again, deliberately. Until something happens that reminds us, yet again. Until we forget again, deliberately. Again. A cycle.

What happens if we deliberately choose not to forget? What happens if we deliberately choose to focus on Him every day, moment by moment? Then when things come our way, we are already in the center of His will. We are not knocked off balance; rather, we are held in the center of His grace.

185

How many times has something rocked your world and reminded you where your focus should be? We don't need an event to prompt change. Deliberately choose not to forget. This is a choice.

The Waters 2 Peter 3:6

By these waters also the world of that time was deluged and destroyed.

These were the same waters that God created.

The same waters that covered the expanse of the earth were used to destroy the wickedness within. I cannot even fathom the chaos and confusion of that day. The surprise at the rain that quickly turned into disbelief and denial that led to the realization that the rain wasn't stopping. Then utter despair filled their hearts as they each personally realized that life as they knew it was coming to an end.

I imagine the day the rain started began as any other day. There were blessings and hardships, laughter and tears, births and deaths; and only He knew what was to happen on that day. He had chosen Noah and his family because of the manner in which they lived their lives. He knew their hearts and set their lives aside from the destruction. He found them worthy.

I want to be like Noah, awake and listening to His voice. I am afraid that satan encourages us to be lulled into lives of complacency. Some of us have lives that are relatively good with very little turmoil. We walk each day fully embracing our "many blessings" from God without ever truly knowing His Face, His Hand and His Voice. We assume since "it" is good, "it" is from God, because "only bad things come from satan." Right? Or maybe, quite possibly, satan doles out evil disguised as goodness. A shiny piece of fruit, perhaps?

While we should enjoy our blessings and cherish the happiness we receive from them, we should be cautious to see beyond tangible rewards. For those from God, treasure them. Remember them and be thankful for each and every one. Instead of seeking blessings, seek His Kingdom, for what is here is only temporary. Listen to His Voice.

Seek Him.

Destruction 2 Peter 3:7

By the same word the present heavens and earth are reserved for fire, being kept for the day of judgment and destruction of the ungodly.

Fire. The first judgment of the world was by water and the next will be by fire.

The story of Chicken Little tells of a town crier who, because of an acorn falling from the sky, insists that the sky is falling. Chaos ensues in the farmyard, but the sky does not fall. The end is near. The end is near. Yet, days and nights continue much as they did before. And we become complacent. Repent, for the end is near. Destruction, or at least destruction from God's Hand, seems unfathomable, if not impossible.

So, we pray for His blessings upon our life. We pray for healing when we are sick, we pray for work when none is available, we pray for food, we pray for safe travel. And we continue about our lives as if this world is our main focus. At times, our only focus. We continue on as if our personal comforts are paramount on this life journey. Our journey expands past this world, so our creature comforts aren't the end-all.

See, we aren't chickens misinterpreting destruction by what we have experienced. We aren't operating blindly. Quite the contrary, we are people who have been given the written Word, personal experience and God's visible creation, and they tell us that destruction is coming. No jokes. No exaggerations.

Truth.

There is a battle for souls here. Every moment of every day. We have to rest and regain strength and nourishment to continue. We need personal "me" days to rejuvenate (some of us more than others).

And as we lay aside our swords; as we, in our minds, take ourselves off the battlefield, the battle rages on.

Stand ready. Face reality. Be on guard even during times of rest.

Bound 2 Peter 3:8

But do not forget this one thing, dear friends: With the Lord a day is like a thousand years, and a thousand years are like a day.

Time.

Here on earth, we are bound by it. Sixty seconds equal one minute. Sixty minutes equal one hour. Twenty-four hours equal one day, and seven days equal a week. And time goes on and on.

And if we weren't confined enough by time itself, we challenge ourselves to do as much as possible with our time, thus confining ourselves even more.

Color-coded schedules, day timers and planners, and smart phone alerts are created to allow us to manipulate time as efficiently as possible. And for what?

To be busy? To fill up voids in our lives? To fit in? To be like everyone else? I wonder what our calendars would look like if we took a yellow highlighter and highlighted the events that really mattered. What would it look like if we only highlighted the events we would attend if we knew our time on this earth was limited? Would we find that the majority of our schedule wouldn't even exist? Would we focus on relationships and God and His work? Would we say "no" more often and "yes" when it really matters? Would we take time to know our neighbors, to help when needed and to do it with pure hearts and not out of guilt?

See, our time here is limited. For some of us, this might be our last week, our last year or last decade on this earth. Or possibly, our last day. It is time for us to take control of our time, to choose purposefully and mindfully what we schedule so when that day comes, when our last breath is drawn, we will have spent our last days doing exactly what we were created to do.

When Tae died, I could look at her last year or so on this earth and know that she wouldn't have done a thing differently. Not one. She lived for :Him and only :Him, out of obedience and joy. What a legacy she left, not one of regret, but one of encouragement for those of us still on this journey to make every day a good enough day to be our last.

Standing Ready 2 Peter 3:9

The Lord is not slow in keeping His promise, as some understand slowness. Instead he is patient with you, not wanting anyone to perish, but everyone to come to repentance.

There is a side of me that is ready. Ready for His return right this minute, this instant, this hour, this second, this breath. There is a side of me that selfishly is done with all of the hatred, evil and deceitful behavior. Done with a world decaying, done with false pretenses and teachers of religion. There is a side of me that is selfishly desiring just to catch a glimpse of our daughter in all the glory of heaven, to see my mother without pain, to see the impossible be possible. To rest at my Teacher's feet and to see His face.

Yet, it is not my call.

It is not within my power to call it done, and that is a good thing. For when that day comes, as glorious as it will be for those who have chosen to walk the narrow path, who have chosen Him as Lord of their life, just as devastating will it be for those who have not.

We pray to be more like Him, to be Christ-like, yet, we selfishly wish to rush the end of this time. I don't think those two can go hand-in-hand. I try to imagine being the last believer to believe before the end of this time, the last soul to be saved, the last to escape an eternity of hell. What if it were my soul? And then, I feel the conviction deep within my soul. Shame on me.

God's timing is perfect, and, in that statement, I must find a peace within my soul that says, "Your will be done." Instead of rushing the end, I must strive to see as He sees that each one is worthy to be saved.

Each one.

In the Blink of an Eye 2 Peter 3:10

But the day of the Lord will come like a thief. The heavens will disappear with a roar; the elements will be destroyed by fire, and the earth and everything done in it will be laid bare.

Come like a thief.

We've heard this before. Some of us have heard it so many times it's cliché. Even so, when the time comes, Christ's return will be sudden and swift. The thief doesn't come with a loud processional before his arrival. He works quietly and quickly so as not to cause alarm before he acts. Then when the moment of opportunity becomes apparent, he acts swiftly and decisively, thus increasing his chances of being successful.

The best defense against the thief is to anticipate his coming before he arrives. Plan for it, prepare and mentally be ready. Many have said that Christ won't return, or that He will, but not in their lifetime. On the other hand, there are those who predict specific days and signs to pinpoint His return. His Word is very clear; He will come, and only the Father knows the time.

Our daughter's sudden departure from this earth forever changed my complacency. Quickly and decisively, her life here ended. No warnings, no proclamations. Forever gone from this earth. And yet, truthfully, the warnings and proclamations were communicated long before. He has told us time and time again in His Word, "Be ready." The shock of the phone call quickly gave way to a sense of awesomeness as I watched Scripture unfold. I knew that my daughter was, at that very moment, watching Scripture come to life in the heavenly realm. That she had just stepped into the portion of Scripture we had anticipated, long-awaited and treasured. She was there. Oh glorious day!

We can choose to live a life of complacency. We can choose to go about our days with our heads in the sand, thinking it won't happen in our lifetime, it won't affect me until I'm older, it won't happen in our family. Until it does. And we are caught off-guard, much like the homeowner the thief targets.

192

However, if we purposefully plan for His arrival, if we live knowing He is returning, knowing our time is limited, then we take away one of satan's biggest arsenals: fear. Our Father has told us what is ahead. He has told us that our lives will not be easy. He has warned us that we will face persecution and death. We know. We don't face the unknown.

We face a future that is mapped by the Almighty. We can either choose to study and follow the Mapmaker, or we can choose to wander aimlessly on the map, choosing purposefully not to be enlightened by the Truth. This will end. It will. The day or night will be ordinary and the trumpet will blast. For a moment, close your eyes and imagine that moment. Live ready.

How Radical? 2 Peter 3:11-12a

Since everything will be destroyed in this way, what kind of people ought you to be? You ought to live holy and godly lives as you look forward to the day of God and speed its coming.

Just how radical are we to be?

Isn't that the million-dollar question? Where is the litmus test? What is radical enough for God but not radical enough to be considered irresponsible in this world? Is He really asking us to sell everything and move to serve the poorest of the poor? Is He really asking us to forgo extracurricular sports in order to focus on His mission? Does He really want us to be so different?

I remember reading the book *Radical*. It took me five separate times over two years to finish. I would start and then have to set it down as I contemplated and pondered. I thought I was contemplating and pondering what God really meant when He said, "Follow Me." I now realize I was wrestling with satan and my worldly desires. God's Word is clear. His direction is firm. Follow Me. The contemplating and pondering was me trying to justify not being completely obedient. Living this half-hearted existence as a follower of Christ and a comfortable American. But, what about? But, what if? But, how can I? But, that isn't how it is done. But, but, but.

But, I have noticed that God doesn't change. He is constant. Always. If we allow His Word to penetrate our hearts and minds, we, however, will change. We will start to realize that what the world might call radical, God describes as simple obedience. What this world proclaims as crazy, He proclaims as sane. What this world would give medals and glory for, He turns away. The question isn't, "Just how radical does He want us to be?" The question is, "Whom do we really serve?" And if we say Christ, do our lives reflect the words that we say?

See, if God calls you to do something, if something "radical" comes to mind and you know in your heart of hearts that He has put that desire there, then you simply do. If in the middle of the night, He tells you to call a perfect stranger to ask how they are, you do. If He prompts you to pray specifically for something that seems crazy, get on your knees at that very moment. If He tells you to take food, you do. If He tells you not to, you don't. But how do you know it is God? Is it worldly? Is it selfless? The more you walk in His will, the more you hear His voice clearly. The more you respond in obedience, the more confirmation you will receive.

However, when we choose not to respond, we also receive confirmation. When we find that the person God had prompted you to pray about suddenly has died, when the food that you didn't take meant the difference between starvation and survival, when the friend you didn't call walks away from her family, when we choose, for whatever reason, not to obey, we will also see where we should have obeyed. We will see where we could have been serving in His will. And as we walk further outside of His will, we stop seeing and become blind to His will for our lives, and then we start to believe He isn't listening to us anymore when actually it was us who stopped listening long before.

Live for Him. It isn't radical. It is what we were created to do.

Love is not Forever 2 Peter 3:12b

That day will bring about the destruction of the heavens by fire, and the elements will melt in the heat.

I will never forget the day when I realized my true love and I would not be together forever. I came to realize that there would be a day when our lives, as we know it, would part. Throughout our years of dating and engagement, I spent all of my time and energy anticipating the next time I would see him and waiting for that next milestone. First, the wedding, then the house, then the birth of our children. Then one night as I was reading my Bible, I started to understand the implications of the message. They are more than just words on a page; they are Truth. And as tears fell onto the page, I looked around and knew that all of this, all of it, was just the window dressings of a life on this earth.

Even though I had been a believer for several years, I was just beginning to delve into His word and apply it to my life. A life I loved. A husband I adored. A husband I loved waking up to every day and going to bed with every night. But that night, I realized that what I thought was the final prize in my world was actually just the beginning. I realized that the beginning scenes were prefacing an eternal life that will be so different than the one that we were creating for ourselves on this earth. "But, God, I have exactly what I want right now. This is good." And I remember sensing, "But this is not it."

So, I found myself shying away from the verses and chapters of the Bible that revealed destruction of life as we know it. I focused on Christ's life and His mission to His people and avoided the rest of the story. No matter how hard I tried, I found that I couldn't study part of His Word and reject the rest, for all of It is integral to our faith. Finally, taking a deep breath, I plunged into His Word, this time drinking it all in, not just parts, but all. Destruction and all. And in His Truth, I found Him. All of Him.

I was not meant to worship my husband, my children or my career. They have been given to me as blessings and are not to be placed above God. Sunday became a day to worship my Savior corporately, but these days paled in comparison to the worship that became a part of my everyday life. Just me and His Throne. My confidence was no longer found in earthly things but in the King, and, through this, I found freedom. I found that this life, as precious as it is, can be as tragic as it appears, and as fleeting in its purpose. This is not it. It isn't. Tomorrow will come as God allows it to come. My job is to prepare for it, but He ordains it to be. Not me. By "carrying the weight of the world on my shoulders," I am just humoring myself as to just how much power and control I have. I really carry nothing on my shoulders, for He carries it all.

While I am my husband's wife and true love, I am most importantly His helpmate in this world. Together, we face a spiritual battle every day. I can either be a help or a hindrance. I can either be a solution or a problem. Am I worthy of this calling to be a wife? For my children, I am the first reflection of Christ that they will see on this earth. I am the only reflection of Christ they will see lived out behind closed doors. Am I worthy of this calling to be a mother?

In the beginning, I was far from it. Focused only on things that would have burned quickly in the fire. Today, I am learning to focus on those eternal things. We've been granted another morning on this earth; may we use it wisely and purposefully.

The Door 2 Peter 3:13

But in keeping with his promise we are looking forward to a new heaven and a new earth, where righteousness dwells.

You see, death is just the door. The next step, if you will, into eternity. We cling to the life that we know. We cling to the busyness and craziness of a world that, no matter how hard we try, will never, ever make sense. We can try to force it. We can twist it and spin it to where it is "doable" but there comes a point when, frankly, it can't be spun anymore. A point at which we bow our heads, slump our shoulders and say, "I can't carry this anymore."

There comes a point when we realize that the more we work, the harder we try, the more desperately we seek, it simply doesn't add up. In fact, it appears to become even worse than it was before we started. And then we enter into despair. Despair in a world that will encourage our defeat. Despair in a world that will agree all is lost and hope is gone. Despair in a world that will stand beside us as long as we believe that there is no hope and that this life is, in fact, quite possibly meaningless because no matter how we spin it, it ends up that we all die anyway.

So what does it really matter? What does it really matter if we try hard, if we seek improvement, if we work harder, if we shoulder the responsibilities? We all die anyway, yes? And the slippery slope continues as the spiral picks up speed, and we lose whatever control we thought we had.

Yet, within each of us, there is the connection to our Creator. A spark within, sometimes deep within, but ever-present. The desire to know hope, the desire to live forever. Isn't that what the great quest is all about? How to fight death. How to stay young forever. How to live forever. However, instead of reaching out to the One who offers this freely, we brush aside His promptings, push down our innate desires and strive on, trying to make it on our own. Just as satan tempted Eve in the Garden of Eden, "You don't need God.

He just says that you do so you will be enslaved to Him forever," satan whispers in our ears. He encourages us to find our own way so that we serve no one but ourselves, but, in the absence of choosing to serve the One true God, we have chosen to serve another.

This world will never make sense. It just won't. Hunger and poverty, abuse and neglect, sickness and betrayal will always be a part of this world. We can try and try to change it on our own, and we might find some success, but it will be much like the "win" in a casino. It isn't lasting and only feeds our desire to win more. But the moment when we realize this is not a game about us that ends in death for everyone, but a lively battle in which our lives are an intricate part every moment of every day, our eyes will be opened to the realization of Who He is, and each of His promises will become relevant to our lives.

A new heaven and a new earth. His promises are true whether we believe or not.

The Hour I First Believed 2 Peter 3:14

So then, dear friends, since you are looking forward to this, make every effort to be found spotless, blameless and at peace with him.

I remember when I first believed. Really believed. And then I remember the realization of what this would mean for my life if I decided to follow Him. While we weren't "bad" in a worldly sense, there were certain aspects of my life that would need to change. Would they have to change? No, they wouldn't have to. Nobody has to do anything but live and die, right? Or at least this was the argument my mind was having with itself. "But I don't want to. But it really isn't bad. But everyone is doing it. Maybe He doesn't mean literally. I'm not hurting anyone. It is just for fun."

And then, I started studying about His second coming, and I knew that there were certain places I had been going and things I had been doing that I didn't want to be found doing upon His return. Not out of fear but rather out of respect. Not because of a directive but because of my desire to be at peace with Him at all times. This doesn't come easy, and I fail miserably at it sometimes. As the Holy Spirit reminds me Whose I am, I am reminded that it takes effort to be different. It takes effort to be spotless and blameless in this world. And while it is true, very true, that we can't please everyone, it is imperative that we align our lives to please Him and only Him so that we stand on a foundation that is firm and secure. A foundation that doesn't change to suit our will but rather provides a basis to build our will upon.

Effort. Hard Work. Determination and perseverance.

That is what it takes to be spotless, blameless and at peace with Him. It takes work. We don't just happen into it. We don't just coincidentally fall into His will. We must work hard. The key, though, I believe, is in the use of great discernment in the decision about where we focus the sweat of our brow. We can literally work ourselves to the ground in activities, programs and the busyness of this world.

Through this, we accomplish great things, and, yet, we still sometimes find ourselves at odds with someone. Whether it be our family, the people we serve with or the people we serve, somebody, somewhere will be unhappy with what we have done no matter how hard we work. No matter how hard to have tried to create the perfect meal, the perfect holiday, the perfect plan.

However, if we seek to be at peace with Him, to be blameless and spotless in His eyes, we will find a measuring stick that doesn't change. That doesn't seek to hurt us. That doesn't secretly desire to see us fail, but a measure that rejoices in our very creation. Imagine being valued solely for Whose you are. The most incredible thing of all is that we don't have to imagine it. It is real, here for the taking. We just have to accept it. We just have to allow our hearts to be loved unconditionally. A love that truly sets out to guide us to be the best we can be.

Solidarity Through Faith 2 Peter 3:15

Bear in mind that our Lord's patience means salvation, just as our dear brother Paul also wrote you with the wisdom that God gave him.

Peter and Paul.

I love the relationship that exists between these two in Scripture. They both were used by God to write portions of the Word, but their writings are diverse. Paul focuses more on salvation and grace, whereas Peter writes more about how we should live. Their words complement each other. To me, they represent how we as Christians should be in our world today. Each of us has been given gifts from the Father to contribute and impart to this world. And, like Paul and Peter, they are all unique and different. Yet even in their differences, they are all centered on the firm foundation of Christ. They point, without contradictions, fully to Him.

Why then do we see so much conflict amongst believers serving God's people? Why do we experience gifts being used, not to reach the lost, but to elevate self as if the gifts are of our own making? Why, instead of encouragement steeped in sisterly and brotherly love, do we see wickedness lightly covered with "sweetness and hospitality?"

We don't need the world to persecute us. We Christians, if we are not careful, do a mighty job ourselves. In our haste to elevate our own deeds, we inadvertently discredit our brother's work. In our desire to be known or to receive credit, we bring a shadow of doubt upon our sister's testimony. In our need to satisfy our fleshly desires, we create adversity where there should only be solidarity. We allow satan to stir amongst our circles. We gossip, we lie, we withhold compliments and encouragement, even when prompted by the Holy Spirit.

We disobey.

We forget that in God's eyes, we can all hold a special place. There isn't just one lead position. Everybody serves a lead position in God's plan. The lead position is what He has given each of us to do, and that position is important, whether it be to lead the masses on this earth or to hold a newborn baby in the nursery. Peter and Paul got this. They were so in awe of their Father that they were wholeheartedly sold out to Him. There wasn't room for any petty grappling between them. They understood that they each were serving the same God, the same purpose, the same faith. Instead of using each other as a stepping stone, they used each other to bring solidarity to our faith. They used our faith to encourage each other in times of adversity.

We have been called to be different from this world. Yet, within our Christian circles, there are many who have been hurt and there are many who have hurt others. It is time to choose to be different and not just model Christianity, but truly live it, down to the smallest detail.

We share a faith that says God places a high value on every soul. Every soul. We proclaim that any presentation of the gospel is success even if just one responds. We celebrate and cheer when salvations occur, but do we mourn likewise when, because of our actions, someone is driven from their position of faith? Do we mourn when we either intentionally or inadvertently cause another pain so that we might feel better?

Encourage one another. Truly encourage one another. I have been pleasantly surprised to find selfless encouragement in some circles where I thought I would find territorialism. True Kingdom-building mentality. Alternately, I have been left speechless when I've stepped into circles expecting deep Christian fellowship, only to find great insecurities leading to turf battles. Battles between believers over "turfs" within our faith! Really? How can we expect the lost world to listen when we proclaim the Truth?

Be different today. Let's search our hearts and ask God to reveal to us where we have been withholding encouragement, and let's encourage. Pray for those God has brought into your world to serve alongside. Together, strengthen the sweet flavor of His Truth so that all might believe.

Just Pray 2 Peter 3:16

He writes the same way in all his letters, speaking in them of these matters. His letters contain some things that are hard to understand, which ignorant and unstable people distort, as they do the other Scriptures, to their own destruction.

Consistency. Blessed assurance.

Throughout time, the message has remained the same. Relevant and constant. Real and unchanging. Every passage in Scripture is complementary to the rest, and there are no contradictions.

Still, we find God's word difficult to understand. We believe ordinary people can't possibly understand His teachings, much less teach others. So, we don't even try. We allow others to interpret His words and messages for us. We never work to contemplate His messages ourselves. We passively listen, thinking we just can't get it.

Some of us even worry about the quality of our prayers and become icy steel if someone calls us out to pray. What if we don't do it right? We worry about the format, the opening, the closing and the in-between.

But you know what is most freeing? When we focus on Him, we find that what is inside of us is good enough. We find that we were created to pray to Him, read His word and put it into practice. Each and every one of us, regardless of our reading level (or even ability to read), regardless of our "lot" in life. This is what we were created to do. Simply created to worship the King.

But satan has always tried to distract us from our Kingdom calling, from our true destiny. He seeks to destroy, and he starts with lies about the integrity of Scripture. He leads us to believe that scriptures that are hard to understand, like those written by Peter, aren't holy, or that we don't have ability to grasp their meaning. This is not true; we can mature in our understanding as we study the whole of Scripture. And all of it— every single verse—is God-breathed.

Stay close to Him. Take a deep breath and pray out loud. I remember my first prayer uttered out loud in front of others. I was scared to death because others prayed so incredibly perfectly, but I remembered I was talking to Him, so "whom shall I fear?"

I have found that God reveals true understanding when I am ready and only when I am ready. God is truly relevant in all things. We just have to relinquish all sense of false control we think we might have and really mean it when we say, "Your will and not my own."

On Guard, Always 2 Peter 3:17

Therefore, dear friends, since you have been forewarned, be on your guard so that you may not be carried away by the error of the lawless and fall from your secure position.

Always, always be on guard.

Satan seeks to discredit, disarm and destroy. He stops at nothing to reach his intended purpose. Wrapping hideous sin in beautiful packaging, enticing believers to stray slightly, he slowly eases his way into our lives. Oh, if only sin visibly looked, smelled and tasted as the evil and wickedness it is. We would not even glance its way, shielding ourselves from the decay it causes. Instead, it glimmers and glitters, and plays with our emotions. And we find ourselves lingering. One touch won't matter, one more word, one more conversation, one more look.

And as we linger, we find ourselves in a moment in time when all seems better in our world. Conflicts are resolved. We feel our needs being met. Our secrets have found a way to get us through the day and night. Unknowingly, we are surrounded by the darkness and whispering lies telling us that no one will understand. So we hide deeper and deeper. Until we find ourselves in such a deep, deep pit of wrong, the lies become our truth. No one will understand how we fell this far. Our salvation is secure; however, our position and testimony of how God can use us in this world is not, and we just wasted it all for what will eventually lead us to our own destruction.

As we start to pull away, satan intensifies the lies, reminding us that there will be no grace or mercy for us. We have fallen too far. Lies that once glittered and filled our self-esteem now reek of emotional abuse, heaping words of disgrace and disappointment on our lives. We are ashamed and feel so alone.

Yet the moment we cry "Jesus," we realize He was there all along. Protecting us when we started on the blind path toward destruction. We find that as we shed Light on the darkness, satan's lies become transparent. We find that while we stumbled, we have not fallen from Our Father's mercy. We find grace and love in other believers who will prayerfully walk with us.

We've been given the gift of salvation. Firm and secure. Thankfully, that is a gift God has sealed, and we as humans can't mess it up once we accept His gift. Yet, the accountability of our witness here on earth, our character, our Christian walk is a free-will choice. Do we spend enough time in God's word, surrounding ourselves with His presence? Do we shy away from the slightest enticement of sin?

Stay on guard always.

Beyond Measure 2 Peter 3:18

But grow in the grace and knowledge of our Lord and Savior Jesus Christ. To him be glory both now and forever! Amen.

Grace and knowledge.

In today's world, it seems that so much emphasis is placed on knowledge and the highest academic degrees, the most literary books read, the largest words and trivia of all kinds. Knowledge, it has been said, is power. To know is to have the power over someone else. We can use knowledge to change lives and extend God's Kingdom, or we can use it for evil. We withhold knowledge to try to keep others less powerful. We dole out knowledge like secrets to be traded to the highest bidder. We seek it so we might seem greater than we truly are.

Peter tells us to grow in grace and knowledge. Not just knowledge, but also grace. God has been merciful on our sinful nature. Through our faith in Him, He extends to us eternal life. Yet, Paul tells us to grow in grace ourselves. He encourages us to extend to others a parallel of the grace we have found in our Heavenly Father. We are to extend loving-kindness, gentleness, humility, goodwill and favor to those with whom we daily interact. We are to love others beyond measure, as He has us. We are to be the peacemakers. We are to be set apart from this world, and this alone will set us far apart.

And this is a choice.

We must choose to forgive those who have wronged us, just as He forgave us. Remember our forgiveness of others and His forgiveness of us is like a drop of mist compared to the magnificent ocean. We grow in grace when we extend loving-kindness to those we do not like, with no agenda. We grow in grace when we choose to encourage and love those with whom we compete for positions and titles. We grow in grace when we realize the purpose of all of this is not about us or what we might earn, but about what we might extend in humility to our fellow man.

It is quite possible the reason we are "competing" for the position with another person is so that he might be introduced to the One True God.

208

It is quite possible we experience conflicts so that our spiritual differences can be brought to light, and Truth spoken in love can prevail. During every interaction and moment in time, we must love with grace so that they might know Him. There are so many things in this world that will compete for our attention. To grow in grace might actually fall under the category of "self-improvement," but how many books do we see dedicated to growing in grace? Every year, when millions make New Year's resolutions, how many will resolve to grow in grace? We spend our time and energy strengthening our physical bodies, broadening our network, improving our position and amassing wealth. But will we spend our time growing in grace? Growing in grace may not offer any worldly accolades, quite possibly, the opposite. We may be seen as weakly, naïve cowards. Many advise us to stand up for ourselves, to honor our name, to demand respect for our position, to be a man or woman. And our flesh agrees with them.

Our flesh prepares for battle. It prepares to defend us. But in our spirit, there is a sense of calm. A gentleness comes from the One Who simply is. And as we turn toward Him, we find that our issues begin to dissipate, and, if we allow ourselves to linger in His Truth, we gather the strength to offer grace time after time. We find that offering grace doesn't mean we are weak, but that we are stronger than we ever imagined, and we find peace from the complexities of this world.

I love the lyrics to Matt Redman's song: "Oh the wonderful cross, oh the wonderful cross bids me come and die and find that I can truly live." I have found that to be so true. As I slowly release the trappings of this world, sometimes prying my fingers from their grip; upon release, I find I am no longer hostage to them. I find freedom.

209

Today is the last day.

This was the last Scripture reference that our daughter left us when she gave her best friend a journal with a list of verses to read a year before her passing. This has been such a journey. A journey of death, life after death, real versus superficial belief and then, how we should carry on. Taellor's death has changed me in a way that I would have never imagined, deepened who I really am. It made me reach deeper towards my God in a way that I had not even when I thought that I had. Moreover, through it all we can say, that He is faithful, always.

So after today, we can carry on. We will start in 1 Timothy as we continue to walk in obedience. You are having read this book and the one to follow only by the grace of God. I am still speechless in how He has orchestrated this one, and by the encouragement of so many of you, working on a book proposal. We were in the States for a quick visit and I met with a dear friend of mine who encouraged me once again to put this all in writing. My response was simply that I do not know the publishing world and if this is God's will then He will have to open the doors and walk me step by step. The next day, I found myself being asked if I would consider publishing our journey.

So thank each of you for your encouragement, prayers and unwavering support as we continue on a journey. The book will contains all the writings since Tae's death as we walked through the valley. A follow up book will extend for a full year and up to the without her life on this earth. Again, even as I type these, I am amazed. The proceeds from the book will be used to help support our ministry in the field and Project H.O.P.E. What an amazing answer to prayer! I ask for each of your prayers in this endeavor. We serve an amazing God.

Therefore, tomorrow, we straighten our shoulders and we carry on.

A Year of Obedience contains the completion of one whole year through the valley. We can and we will survive this walk. One step, one breath at a time. Obedient.

Project H.O.P.E.

Project H.O.P.E. is an inter-denominational service organization dedicated to meeting the immediate physical needs of impoverished people, while sharing with them the Good News of Jesus Christ. Serving the poorest of the poor in Nicaragua and Haiti, Project H.O.P.E. strives to serve so that everyone might know Him.

In 1998, Project H.O.P.E. was established after a group of friends felt God calling them to help the poor in Nicaragua. The founding directors had been traveling to Nicaragua for a few years, but felt called to do more than build homes and return to the United States. There was a need to share the Gospel with the people of Nicaragua.

Project H.O.P.E.'s very humble beginning consisted of the directors and their wives traveling to Nicaragua and slowly others joined. Some trips consisted of camping in the mountains and bathing in the river. God has blessed Project H.O.P.E. greatly. Over 700 people travel with Project H.O.P.E. each year. A full-functioning base camp, H.O.P.E. Central Nicaragua was built in 2006. In 2013, we began construction at H.O.P.E. Central Haiti. Both facilities serve as a headquarters for our in-country staff and housing for short-term mission teams.

For those that are interested in a personal boots-on-the-ground mission experience, contact Project H.O.P.E. at pjhope.org and come serve with us bringing Matthew 25:35-36 to life.

For I was hungry and you gave me something to eat, I was thirsty and you gave me something to drink, I was a stranger and you invited me in, I needed clothes and you clothed me, I was sick and you looked after me, I was in prison and you came to visit me.

Taellor's House

Serving as an outreach to <u>single mothers and their children</u>, Taellor's House provides after school care for children along with various programs for mothers. Many school-age children are unable to attend school because they are taking care of their younger siblings while their mother is at work. Taellor's House will provide care for preschool children as well, allowing the older children to attend school.

Children will receive lunch (Monday-Friday), tutoring, biblical teaching, English classes, a school uniform, and school supplies. Mothers will receive biblical parenting skills, vocational skills, and help securing a job. Taellor's House will begin operation in 2016. Internship opportunities are also be available for girls over the age of 18 who are interested in long-term mission work.

Taellor's House is named after Taellor Stearns, who passed away in June 2014 at the age of 19. She was a missionary to Nicaragua and part of the Project H.O.P.E. family. Taellor had a passion for children and was excited about the children's center project. It was only fitting that the center was named after her.

For those interested in hearing more about Taellor's House or intern positions, contact Project H.O.P.E. at pjhope.org.

I remember so vividly the night that Taellor died. So vividly. I remember coming home, telling Slaton, greeting the friends who had come to walk the journey with us, going to my room and as the boys lay sleeping, I remember thinking, "How?"

"How will I ever leave them alone again? How will I ever serve You to my wild abandonment? How will I ever laugh again? How will I ever feel joy again? How will I ever face a world that is so tainted in death? How will I trust again? How will I ever just be again? How can I breath normally? How will I ever answer my phone again? How can I see past the tears and hurt? How can I be who You have created me to be through this?"

And I remember thinking, quite selfishly...., "I will so miss this name, Father. A name You gave us, as unique as she was created, it will be forever gone."

And as satan, true to form, kept whispering doubts, God kept directing me to Psalm 139, He knew. He knew the number of her days. He knew them before she was ever born.

This journey that we walk is a journey that, as those who are walking it also, is not easy. It is an every day, sometimes, every moment, every breath battle. It will be until the day I meet my Savior face to face. It will just be. A battle not between flesh and blood but in the spiritual realm. A battle in which God has remained ever faithful.

He has shown us how to find joy again. How to laugh, even amongst tears perhaps, but how to laugh, how to serve with wild abandonment, how to set it all aside, even amidst the fear and worry, and say, "This is all Yours...and not just say it but to take action upon it." As I've responded before, even as you observe our walk of obedience, make no mistake, I miss her more than there are stars in the sky or sands upon the earth. The smile, the laughter, the wittiness, the servant, the daughter, the friend...yet, God has given us continual peace that none of that has been lost to us but is now being experienced fully in all the splendors of heaven.

And as icing on the cake, just because He can, He has taken that name that He bestowed on her so uniquely and is using it daily to bring Hope. When I see it, when I type it, I don't feel pride nor entitlement, but rather I feel the magnitude of His grace and mercy as He does what only He can do. The name no longer simply represents a young girl that solely wanted to serve her King by loving on the children He placed before her but rather represents His Hand, His Mighty Hand upon this earth.

Absolutely breathtaking.

Thank you for walking this journey with us. We chose to publish this book independently in order to maintain the original writings just as they were written when we were daily walking the journey through our valley of death. Words written raw everyday. Words written through tears and unspeakable pain. Yet, words that brought comfort and joy as God continued to be faithful. The devotions continue through the first year after her death in Live Worthy due out winter 2017.

You can continue to follow our journey at Tammy Conner Stearns on Facebook or contact us at stearnstammy@ymail.com to share your own journey.

I am also available for speaking engagements.

May we find Hope through Him always.

Made in the USA
Coppell, TX
14 October 2021

64048279R00128